Poetic Love Frenzy

"Break free from the labels that define you."

Connecting Mind, Body, and Soul through
Truth Tales Shared in Love

Written and created by Shanna Rebis

Inspired by her faith in God

PAGE PUBLISHING, INC.
New York, NY

First originally published by Page Publishing, Inc. 2016

ISBN 978-1-68348-456-1 (Paperback)
ISBN 978-1-68348-457-8 (Digital)

Printed in the United States of America

FOREWORD

W*ho is Shanna Rebis?*

And what makes Shanna tick?

Since I've known her, Shanna runs on intuition and emotion. Trusting her "gut" has served her well. Please don't think that means her life has been easy. Shanna has faced hard choices, made some bad decisions and some good ones. She's failed and succeeded in personal relationships and in business, suffering grave losses and amazing successes.

If there is one constant in Shanna's life, it has been a deep caring, especially for those who may have lost hope or don't remember who they are or who they want to be.

And Shanna has turned that into a career as a life coach, training people's minds as well as their bodies, helping others to acknowledge how extraordinary, beautiful, and intelligent they are and showing them that love resides in them no matter how lost, dark, hurt, or alone they may be.

Shanna's passion is to inspire others to find peace and truth in their own lives and encourage them to heal their inner selves. She does not claim to have all the answers, but she is able to connect on a primeval level that resonates through you like a soft wind through chimes.

In *Poetic Love Frenzy*, Shanna shares her journey with pride. She is neither ashamed nor afraid of the twists and turns her life has taken. She welcomes the grief as well as the glory. "Without pain," says Shanna, "there is no glory to be known." Shanna offers you her love story and perhaps more importantly, she gives you the tools to make your life your own.

Nicoletta Barrie
Author, Editor, and Beloved Aunt

DEDICATION

To Yolanda Mary Ventura Rebis, otherwise known as my grama. A life force whom has had a most profound influence in my life, even now as she watches over me and our family. I give great thanks to her for guiding me through writing this book. *She is my angel.* This woman whom has inspired me, given me courage, showed me the way, in being love and what it truly means to tell the truth. Not by telling me but by her actions and her undying Faith and love for GOD. Because of her, I dedicate all of who I am in light of her unconditional love.

A special and sincere thank you to my parents whom always act upon true love.

To my brother whom was my very first best friend and today I am proud of the man who stands tall for all its worth. Way to go!

To the baby, the child, the li'l one who came and went in a moment time, just enough time for me to feel what it is to be a mommy. *In love you were made and in love you remain.*

To Moonie, words and style . . . Memories withstand all that is lost. *For I will always love you, as if you were my daughter.*

To Janelle, my goddaughter. I am so proud of you and the realism you portray—it is the magic!

To the dear ones who encouraged me to write a book!

To Aunt Niki for your confidence and unconditional love, always.

To family, friends, acquaintances, and strangers too, if you have entered my life for a moment or for a lifetime spent, in my heart I pray for you. Know your worth for this life is Amazing Grace, *because of you.*

Special thanks to my husband, because of your patience and genuine kind nature. I remember what is most important, *again!* All of you whom came into my life and made an incredible impact—you know who you are.
Thank you with my whole heart, in being love.

"Kindness our passage on the path to enlightening Peace."

PREFACE

If for any other reason, my life has gone in a direction and somehow made me more grateful, more satisfied and somehow brought an overwhelming feeling to help bring light to the world so they may come to understanding love, in being. To *know hope* is never farther from a glance over our shoulder or in the smile of a child, a voice that utters sweet tomorrows. That it tis never over, in truth it is just the beginning. So you see my friend when your Faith is wilted like a flower in Fall, this is your time to let it all go, so all may be renewed, healed and brought whole again in the wake of springtime, as whistled yesterday's give *a promise*, love was here and it now blooms wildflowers, and good afternoons to anyone and everyone. Walk your bare feet through the green grass, feel the wind blow through you and in a deep breath in search of something—well this is the time, so go forth with your journey. Venture, with love as your guide and hope as your friend. Faith will lead, always trust when the halls start to darken and all seems lost forever more, a road will open up to you, follow it true. A prayer I send in a basket so open when you are hungry and in need of soul. May it feed you and supply you with depths of everlasting beats, tune in and all will be right, as you make room, every step that you take with all of your might.

"Life is a puzzle and we the pieces."

In a world where social media has become our new best friend, bringing us closer and connecting all of us. I saw this as a window and opened it wide. I felt it was a great opportunity, a way to use my voice, a good source of attention and observation in getting to know people and myself on a different level, and a time to make things right in a positive way. It started out as a networking tool and soon I found myself journaling poetry, thoughts, and feelings about love. It allowed me to express in a freeway, and through acknowledging real and sensitive issues, I inspired a community of positive and insightful trend to grow love awareness not just for me but for others whom share in with the idea "the good life within." It all started in 2011, but positive enlightenment energy is still growing today. So *Poetic Love Frenzy* is born to the public.

The *journal read* you are about to discover is true in theory and raw in nature, creatively written with love as my guide. Take it in with all your heart. The intent is for you to enjoy and even share. The words have healed, transformed, and even come to engage brilliance in wonder again.

Be noble in your step and humble in your words.
"Be Love"

Unplug from your network and be in tune with the music that plays all around you, just for you.

May this book breathe new life into your lungs, heal your heart from the pain, and give you momentum to try again because you are worth it!

Poetic Love Frenzy is meant to inspire as it has inspired me to heal and succeed many times over.

I now reside with my family, in Florida, a dream of thirteen years. I want others to know there is hope, and it does only take one person to make the world better. Proving the theorem true.
"Blooming like a wildflower in a garden of love."

Make room for the light . . .

Photo taken by Shanna, empowering a positive notion that a miracle of heaven is present.

The sun opens her arms, and his light reaches out . . . Radiating magic, blessings, healing, and love.

CHAPTER 1

Inspiring Love

"Inspire what comes from the heart."

Manifesting love vibes is a practice we must act upon in our daily lives. Wanting peace in your life is simply not enough you have to be willing to do the work that is necessary of you. The wanting, the wishing—it is the first realization, to having the good life within.

The genie in the bottle only grants us the very things we work toward, in faith *and* perseverance.

Brand your love and align your thoughts with *action*.

When you are confronted by another, give them eye contact. Let them know you care enough to listen to what it is they have to say. People deserve respect. Why would you deprive yourself of something so special?

A live connection = Peace within, perfection

A very key component in *"connecting mind, body and soul"*

"Be Love"

In translation, to be in a love state.

Reinstating heart back into our lives **is** my motivation. What is yours?

On a journey still looking for what truly matters. Getting closer, each moment brings me eternal peace. Standing taller, each truth I tell, love reveals ultimate happiness inside my soul, a knowing for what is ahead. Making room for the light.

Align with the universe as you are a star in the galaxy visiting a place of experience.

We must envision. See what it is we need. It is not always what we want. Wanting is most the time what we see on the outside, in the lives of others. What they have and how they perceive themselves to the world projects onto society standards of what is true and what is right in a sense of possessions, materials, physical beauty, and wealth in financial status. Even their relationships look better from where you stand. But to judge fellow man or merely covet another's things is a sabotage to one's truth and what is good for you.

To be truly gracious for one's happy life is an unselfish act. For instance, to have no thoughts on what is better nor worse and to have an appreciation for a beautiful piece of art, a view over the lake, taking landscape in a land three thousand miles away from the comforts of home. There are so many miraculous and sound discoveries if you only take notice.

Most of the time, people concentrate on the end result of a friend, colleague or stranger's success, or their own for that matter. Rarely do they find appreciation and take in each beautiful moment in the making of all creation.

Just be. Gravitate toward *your* happy. For me it is taking in many cultures, breathing in love, the wondrous body of nature and every aspect of what defines art and *delicious desserts* for they have my taste buds dancing, *for the very thought of chocolate excites me!* There are so many wonderful blessings to be thankful for. I would have you here on this very paragraph all day.

How could one choose only one favorite color when each mood brings on a different feeling—blue, green, yellow, to name a few. A rainbow is proof there is color to be seen and felt. "*I want all of them, for I am.*"

Everything is luminous, free, and willing to offer treasures to whomever lavish in truth, so be it. *It is yours.* The circle of all life, whatever you so choose to live.

Time travel: close your eyes and believe *with* faith, work on your part and courage. *Anything is possible!*

"All the world's a stage." Play for me, dance for me, dress for me, but I know myself to be true. This can be mistaken for what it is we truly need to be happy. What is meant to be enjoyed and always inspired.

False witness is being construed by the audience. *In meaning*, the lack of security and love within the people has led to a chaotic distraction, crazy illusion of what is real and what is right. I see this displacement everywhere. We glamorize sex in a way that portrays anger and greed. This indecency that is being exposed is not intimacy if it is driven by hate.

Ask yourself who intentionally vows of this type of life. How do they feel deep down within, at home alone at night? For to choose this is one thing but with absence of truth, love and feeling is void. Well, that is just it my friends.

Our Life Is Awaiting for Us to Be

In precedence with my intuitive self and shared experience, I see through the pain that leads to the dark side. People are afraid to feel yet are more abused and used by not facing their feelings and avoiding at all costs the truth. Vulnerability into the dark, eluted by those controlling the will of souls with whom have no voice, nor confidence. Bending their love for what gifts they have instilled in them naturally, using money as a tool or vice, excuse even. To take and swindle their God-given talents and lie to the public. And worse, the public believes no harm is done.

You see the mass production of injured souls that have been neglected are being abused by a dark and alluring culture. It is in us, *the need for love.* That is why when we do not have it in our life, we become weak and vulnerable to empty desire, lies, and control mongers.

In life sometimes, we have to walk through a story to become the very person we are meant to be. It is a dangerous walk for I have walked this line. I assure you it is short-lived. I will tell that story one day, but for now, *I express to you* that eternal happiness *comes from some place* much richer than anything. It elevates us higher, leaving us invigorated and eager to know more, *to be more*. There is no emptiness on this journey, but I do warn you. You will need *stamina* in your *will* and *strength* in your *heart*.

Being in the very moment of existence
The difference in *being* and *existing* is that alone.

Pre-meditation is a practice, an intent to be a true being in conscious thought

When we are present and thought-conscious in our daily lives, then we have the opportunity to mend and feed the very souls of those we come in contact with. To be honest, it is when I am good to myself that I have this amazing ability to help others—whether it is patiently waiting in line at the supermarket or at a local coffee shop or maybe at home with my family, wherever it may be.

I also have found when life trips me and my plans are broken by mistakes made or natural occurrences take place, if it is on my part or someone else's, always I am lead to a chance meeting, or remarkable fate, that changes me for the better, *every time*. In the hustle of everyday life, we seem to come undone when we are standing still. When five minutes feels like twenty minutes. We are provoked to act out, and this causes a negative magnetic occurrence.

I was tired of being in a hurry, going nowhere, and treating others unkindly all because I was in a hurry—*what the heck was I thinking!* I was not, and that is my point here. So when I began practicing this method of premeditation in a public place, I realized that this magnetism is in fact true! I found the more I was in tune with my very present moment I was aware of others in a sincere, and personal way, granted the effect of ignorance is up close and personal—you notice everything it seems.

Some will find no reward in your kindness and this might annoy you as it does me on emotional days. But I urge you to look away and pray for them for we do not know the ill others face, and just maybe they need love in a very bad way so smile anyway and walk.

Brilliance in being present, there is a relaxation process that is so worth it.

Timing was now on my side, and I was never late but just *in time* for what was there, meant for me to take notice—the good, the kind, the ones in need of a smiling face. I feel blessed to have the ability to observe what is truly needed and *want* to create positive energy in which my calmness is noticed, received, and continued on by others.

Energy It *tis* Magnetic

Choose to inspire, empower, and rebuild yourself, in doing that you make room for others to be light. A Force you have within you.

Empower your good side and you will be free of *Anxiety, anger, sadness, and stress-related evils.*

"In being, God Connected You Will Have Peace."

Tune inward, my friends. You have an inner compass of faith—draw from it. It will set you up on your road to understanding why you are here and who you are. Learn what it is to truly immerse yourself in truth. You have heard, *"The truth hurts but it will set you free."* It is true. You cannot be born unto a rock; therefore, do not be dense in your thinking. Without meeting truth at each fork in the road, head on. You will be persuaded by doubt and find yourself down a path of consequence, more hurt than you can possibly know or even lead down to a dead end. It will only take you longer to find your true identity.

Why prolong happiness?

Spiritual Awakening

Have you the feeling of being incomplete? Lost? Most importantly, trapped in a body, feeling that a stranger has taken your place? Maybe nobody understands you? Tired of being misunderstood? Don't quite feel like yourself? *Who are you?*

This is maybe why you are reading this book. *What compelled you?* You see, you have already begun seeking. I, at this very moment, feel connected to you—the reader, the being who is a stranger at that. Something has *compelled* me to write this very book and finish, in a timely manner for people who need direction to instill self-worth. I am so blessed for those who have *helped me, guided me, challenged me, inspired me.* For a girl who never liked the everyday school has come to love Earth school.

To change is to merely improve one's version of self. To love you simply because you are a miracle. To find love within is a journey we make through one another.

Find your key note and use your voice.

I am

In short, a bio blurb

I, myself, have come full circle. Over twenty years in working with all types of individuals, I have been truly loving what it 'tis I do! In a way, I have been coaching most of my life—now providing knowledge and wisdom as a life coach.

I tend to get personal, always going over and beyond, and this has created a circle of trust with my clients. Experience is by far our best teacher, and I, a good student. I have been through much pain—from relationships through health related issues. I believe in order to help others, you have to know where they have been emotionally. I also have known much happiness and therefore feel I have the right to state the obvious! I am passionate about life and people; it is my career along as my life purpose.

What sets me aside from another is helping oneself in a space where judgment is not welcomed nor do I find just cause in treating another less than, no matter what the circumstance! Second, I am open and show love unconditionally toward people. We all fall short at times as we all have the ability to climb as high as we believe we can.

"I am not perfect nor better than just one whom has awaken."

Making Every Moment Count
Inspiring Hope, Love, and Compassion to *All Whom Seek*
Writing, Speaking, and Living the Raw and Beautiful Truth
Living the Life God Wants for Me
While I Have Been Hurt, I Still Have a Beating Heart
I Love More Now than I Ever Knew Possible
An Open Heart Loves True
For the Secrets of My Soul *whisper healing notes*
I
Again Free to Live Happily Within My Sacred Self
Touching the Living with Inspirational Thought
Embracing My True Identity
Confidently Challenging Others to Make Room for the Light

"Trust in Your Gut *and* Follow Your Heart."

Just keep moving whatever the reason may be

- Richer and healthier relationships
- Self-improvement
- Forgiveness
- Mindfulness
- Happiness
- True Love
- Purpose
- Religion
- Health
- Peace
- GOD

There are many reasons to name but you get the idea.

Best of love to you, always. Know you *can* and *will do this*. I have dedicated my life to purpose and I believe in you even if you don't just yet. I did not always have the right idea, it took many falls and failures which I am thankful. For I would not be who I am today instilling my purpose. Strong in my character and confident in my words for . . . I am.

"My heart bleeds as yours my friend for I do not know you, but I believe you know heartbreak as I."

"I too fall, but I endure the pain and continue to find a better way to live."

Know, in short, there is no right or wrong way on your journey, but there is a divine timing and you will know of it when you have come to trust in your guide. You ask what guide. I cannot tell you this. It would mean nothing to you at this time. "Trust in yourself and by being attentive, *you will find everything you seek."*

In today's social environment, an age where everything is at our fingertips, we can buy anything we desire and even persuade most to give to us. But in the realm of purpose, we must seek the treasures for ourselves.

Every soul we meet, each experience we endure, every hurt we feel, love leaves an impression on our heart. In all challenges we meet, obstacles that cross our way, love will direct us on our path, appearing as our life map, if you will.

There is no easier way, *except the challenge*. Get out of your own way and on the right road to discovering why you are here. Master your skills so you may apply them in a way—that is meant to be.

"Love is the magic we know as a child."

Be the great inventor you know yourself to be.
Brainstorm unto a new tomorrow for ideas reside in you.
Capable you are.
"Be love."
Restore love to its natural state.
For tomorrow is awaiting you.

Capable you are, and meant you shall be.

When we invite strangers into our lives for the mere sake of learning what it is to be *love*.

Ask yourself is he a stranger or an enemy? *What talk is this*, has it been programmed or perhaps a negative experience trapped you in contempt to think ill of a fellow man? For a family may be divided by hate but th*e one man who stands up and pronounces his fate unto love*, he may be forgiven and spared from deceit. It is in the courage to stand alone, holding your heart for the beast may devour you on sight. As it is in the beginning, as it is now—for that man *be love* and I so choose to stand with him not behind nor in front.

Come to love Angelic moments.
Be present so you do not miss them!

When we neglect the true importance of life from space, time, religion, tradition, culture, race, breed or land, we miss out on the true connection we all long for. Deny it all you want, no living being is separate in love only indifferent in the sense of being. For I am love, I am energy, I am you through your reflection in my mind's eye, so be good because when you look at me, it will be your actions you see looking back at you.

A mirror of man sees himself through the eyes of truth.

May it be *the one* you are looking for
Be present, be true to yourself
Ignore the hate you hear
Listen with a pure of heart
Away with the convictions that make for haste
The love that yearns for open space
Must it be felt and renewed in spirit

Photo taken by Shanna in South Florida

I came across this duck friend whom has taken residence along with others. He spread his wings for me one day in passing, from a morning walk and this inspired me to think twice about ducks and how they too are angelic in nature, offering peace. In knowing angels of heaven still walk this Earth brings great comfort to me.

CHAPTER 2

Love of Self

Breathe in Through Your Heart ♥

Do you ever just breathe intentionally?
At this very moment become con-
scious of your breath, every intake.
Breathe in then out
Feel the way it moves through you.
How very precious the idea of being alive is.
Think about this for a moment.

In awakening you will come to find your will through con-
scious thought. On your journey you will be free in your choices
but remember they are yours' alone to make.

Take the risk for chance is all you've got.

"*Believe in the self. Deep down its roots lay beyond the stars that give
you hope.*"

If you find yourself *alone, confused, lost, or doubtful,*
look up and breathe in through your heart and be still, be present.
I promise you if you have made it this far,
It is normal that these feelings will come about.
The closer you get to the light,
the harder time the dark will have to keep you asleep and miserable.
So breathe in through your heart and trust in the light to carry you through.

Loving yourself is the most important journey you will ever come to make.

Family, Earth Guides, *and* Angels

New school teaches us that we have a choice—granted this is not a new sentiment, remember the circle of life. But keeping it simple, I am forty years young, and when I was growing up, I did not see the view from where I was, flowing through life and later drifting. I stumbled in the dark with crazy eyes and unchanneled energy, up until my experience with life, something of a powerful force, urged me to engage in raw and uncensored living, with part of myself I did not know existed. I like to think of her as another personality that emerged, protecting me for the greater good of my sacred being.

The challenges I faced in those hard and cold days, *for what seemed like eternity,* brought me to life.
Through my pain and heartache did I start to see a truer version of reality in itself. My perception had changed, and there was no turning back to my earlier self. The personality who had stepped in was also gone, vanished without a trace.

"Everything happens for a reason," I heard my mother say in my head. So there it was. Why was this happening to me—pain, abuse, neglect of love, *anger*? I accepted the challenge as I trusted my faith and knew it must have good intention for me and it was up to me to pay attention and grow stronger within myself.

The turmoil is what saved me in an odd way. I accept it for what it is, blaming no one, only do I thank God for the positive influence it left on my *heart, my mind,* and my *soul.*

With conscious thought I elevated higher by soul searching the answers, reading books, teaching myself how to meditate. I began to search for the real meaning of life, love, and death. *On my journey, I came across authentic love for God,* on my way I found me. "Authentic reckoning."

The search for something more in depth had begun to enlighten my broad view, my beliefs, and a sure sense, for suddenly, people, faces and places became unfamiliar and no longer did I feel I belonged to anyone or anything.

Later, seeing others existing in their imitation of life, acting out, in an idea, repeating in the program or following in tradition. When I came to realize this may no longer be a chosen reality in which lead me to slow myself down and take the time to pay attention to that yearning in my own heart the prevailing would free my sacred self from angst, in living a divine truth made especially for me. Sometimes in life it is necessary to rewire our mind. I was not aware that i was reflecting an old version of self and it was time to make my life purpose count for something more in depth than what fraction in the matrix I previously played a part in. I thought of myself strong in my character, romanticizing in my imagination more important active in life. I was raised with an attitude that when you fall, you get back up and do it again!

Yet this time I would be awake!

Love than *love more.*

My parents had instilled a strong sense of faith in me. I thank them for their sacrifices, undying love, and never ending support to this day. But there being a mentality in which they grew up in that everything happens for a reason, you must be happy for what you do have, and having an idea that some have more and some simply was not enough for me. I was to break the cycle and challenge everything as I knew it. In my heart I felt there was more for me than accepting the cards dealt granted I had a great hand!

"Telling me to be happy for what you do have, *Shanna*."
"When you fall sick, go to the doctor. Don't cry about it do something about it!"

You see, they taught me these very skills by addressing what was the truth. It was up to me to find what the truth was and what it meant. I had to discover it for myself. *A freakin puzzle*, of course! I laugh when I think about life and the bigger picture. All that time, I thought that black cloud was for me. All I had to do is dream of a rainbow or not feel sorry for myself. I stopped taking everything personally. Anyway, I find great delight in what it truly means to listen and not just accept what is given to you.

"Words are the pieces the heart connects later."

Little did I know, it was my outside world that I saw this false reality in which we do not have a choice and I had been encircled in a family of one love and given the opportunity to be anything or anyone I want to be, endless amounts of choice.

"For given a choice would you settle for average or accept the challenge and seek more love?"

"Penetrate good thought
Speak words that create positive confident vibes
For if you do not, fear will cultivate misery unto you."

I can remember words my parents and grandparents said to me that stuck. "I mention words and not the actual conversation because the words are what stuck for me, like a switch going off in my head." Words have always intrigued me and made a difference in my life at every turn. There are the words someone gave me, that instilled brilliance, love, thought, change, remorse. With them knowing it or not, *I thank them* and I love who I am, that I listened. I have taken in count, from loved ones, strangers, acquaintances even so-called enemies, the blessings they have shared with me, from afar or next door in some way or another. Words, smiles, and love had assisted in my growing. I do believe there are no coincidences, and I know in my gut that it is my choice to become greater than the demise most succumb to.

"When you think no one is listening or paying attention . . ."

The magic in words would sometimes be stored and applied later when the time was right.

My father, knowing I had a special purpose, prepped me all along and pushed me to always succeed, not in a way meant to control but more of an urge to guide me straight. He did not want me to follow in the same fear of failure. His truth in wanting a better and easier life for me. To act upon my talents and gifts, to not be afraid or lead to believe I am not good enough, but in fact, he had me to believe that I was good enough. My father is the king of ideas—great ones, I will add. He is a brilliant and talented being, wise in a sense of luminous and humble agility. Wholehearted with integrity and creativity to fit. A man good at many frames of life, always aspiring young men to lead by example, unintentionally. Little would he admit to acknowledging credit due. My father is a man of great intent, heart, and work ethic.

He had me to believe *that I was to make for a golden road and follow it true.* He saw something in me and gave me all his wisdom along with tough love I would need to know inside myself, to in fact recognize my potential without presence of ego. He taught me how to discipline myself in spirit, to be strong against evil-driven droids. I know myself to be true and good hearted, as I am special and I have purpose, so when I get lazy or when I lose my faith, his strength is there to remind me to return to stage and do what it is I need to do, in a state of truth.

"When a child is born there comes a truth and this very truth must be seen by the parents so later the parents and child may be spared from sorrow. Those whom are strong in their faith and choose to walk with divine truthness they will be gifted plenty in peaceful bliss—knowing a greater plan is beyond themselves."

Grama had a fearless love for nature and her family. She had a confidence that I admired and wanted to ambulate on to myself, in my life. She was a healer, an empath, and as the heavens would have it, I was just like her. I admired her smile and her presence in a world that tried to break, control, and change her, yet she was protected by something stronger and more beautiful—God and his angels—I presume. I can recall many times her faith saving her and her loved ones. That power of faith and love continue to protect and guide our family.

My Nani taught me things in her own quiet way. I was intrigued in the idea—my grandparents' relationship that is. I was fathomed by the years of togetherness and history they shared in good and bad. The home they shared secured deeper meaning, and I wanted it for my life. One day, sitting in the living room, I asked, *"What is love, Nani,* and how do you know when you find it?" She responded, "You will just know. I cannot tell you. It is a knowing." Her very words! That stumped me and *indeed it was not the answer I was looking for!* Though, I have to admit, it did peak my interest, and from that moment on, I would venture in finding the true meaning of love.

"I would one day embark on a meditative, holy, and sacred truth with God."

Pursuing a dream
having it for a time being
Never far are we
from those whom we love
Born unto the same cosmic space
Gracious in love
Always providing a way
True love resides within me
Walk amongst a dream
in discovering
true self, true life, and true love
Sacrificing material comforts and worldly pleasure
For the will of God would promise me everlasting love
Never without grace
His offerings come to enlighten truth
Entrusted all will be right.

My grandfather was strong in his will. He was a man whom I feared and disliked for many years. I found out later that it was his alcohol abuse that transformed his fear out loud. When he finally quit and changed to be a better man for his family, I found a sincere man full of love, sharing in humor and good food. He was an amazing cook, and his laughter was contagious. He portrayed his weakness, and when he stood up to it and developed a better sense of self, that was the time when all saw him as a great and strong protector of his family. I believe this too. It endowed me the power and inspiration to apply later in life.

"I have an understanding, a compassion for people whom lose sight and I continue to always see the light within them. The individual at will must be ready to commit honesty, also it may be consistent in their timing to recognize—*the light in my eyes is a reflection of the love within them.*"

"My Uncle Bob," who never recovered coming home from Vietnam, was diagnosed as a schizophrenic. I believe he was smart and intuitive, he was kind and generous, he had charisma and character that radiated, *you could not help but adore him*. He, being different after his fate turned, which was a challenge. When we would go out in public people would stare and talk under their breath because he was different, it only reflecting their own fears or lack of understanding, in knowledge or compassion.

"Contagious is man's own voice
lingering in the thoughts of his helpless subjects."

The negative vibes and unkind mumbling made me mad, and I know this is what inspires, empowers, enlivens me. I continue to rebel against the crowd of ignorance. For I now know he was my teacher, my guide, sacrificing his own happiness for mine. Here to show me as a young girl how people are afraid of what they don't know. It would instill me to do something, to make a difference. I was very young and to be subjected to have a uncle with a disability, it was not easy, as you can imagine. I was not always fair to him, for that was my weakness and fear, perhaps, lack of confidence, or mere immaturity. I did good compared to how I could have been. Truth is, he was my hero and still is. The day before he died I was there, as he held my hand and spoke to me telepathically, looking an intense stare right through me, he said, "*I don't want to be here, I want to go home. I need to be free.*" I understood but did not know what it meant at the time.

Trapped

Is the Soul
Who sees only the view from the room of his placed body
Boundless the time and space for one whom sees all possibility
in his mind, body, and soul for he will have plenty of love and richness Beyond measure of a ruler calculated in thoughts of clarity
Add peace as victory for we our of each other no different than
Simply the same in purity.

"Freedom in"

In my present life, I am open to the truth, an inner connection we had, my uncle and I. Being that I am an intuitive, it is why I understood him when others did not. Blessed and very grateful for having this gift that feels like a curse at times, passed down to me and because of the close bond we shared I learned up close, how to care for it, another reason to believe in something more than what I see with my eyes. For life needs to be felt with the heart. I will continue to search my true gifts and listen to my calling.

My family is not perfect for they too are with flaw yet to love them spite their own drama is to be love unconditional.

My mother's words of wisdom: Be proud of where you come from and know who you are, but be better than us. Which meant evolve, learn, grow, explore the world only to come home complete and content.

Genetic traits can hinder new blood lines. By loving unconditionally and becoming in tune to another, we can break the bad habits that have been passed down and work toward achieving the best, in us. In doing this we *can* and *will* lead the future right as life *is* meant to be glorious and joyful.

"My mama" she, a delicate flower. Quiet in nature, among her peers she goes unnoticed, a reflection she carries within herself. Her strength is the very reason I have remained intact and more than willing to survive this lifetime untouched by harm's way. My mother and all her discomfort has brought me to an understanding. For in her struggle I will always tend to a garden and believe you me it will remain utterly beautiful and time will stand still awaiting for my mother's arrival. For her Spirit is Angelic, roaming this earth for the love of her children. Her legend is pure and tenacious, for I would be nothing without her.

I believe my parents, grandparents, and uncle are my eternal earth guides and that I was blessed enough to be challenged by their differences, weaknesses and come to accept their faults and strengths, the magic in my family is what gives, empowers me to be compassionate to others of all ages, to respect those whom have grown old or are different than the societal standard of perfect.

This is my story; yours may be different. Point is, that no matter your story, family, or circumstance, you have people around you and we all have guides and angelic presences to walk with, people of example to teach us, help us, and grow us. Find out how to explore your gifts and abilities. Are you not curious?

Pay attention, you may not always be full of love and fall short in kindness. We are human, and it is in you to choose.

Discover and choose to overcome your fears and live the good life within. "Be love."

"Family"

In all of souls in thy own blood, friends who come close, enemies who challenge our will.

The Guides
who are here
to help us on our path of self discovery
for it is inside the people placed in our everyday
who can change us in a better way
if we only look at it with a clear perspective
Good nor bad we have the choice to see it true.

There are blood ties and invisible bonds that seed us to one.

Photo of my family

We must not misconstrue, manipulate what is. *Be true* in intention and the light will guide you.

See into the darkness, be aware or you will be deceived, only in light can you see in translucency of color, may it lead you out with true vision.

Not knowing reality from illusion and what simply is.

For there is no blame, there is choice in how you choose to see it through truly.

The key to unlocking the secrets will be in the very meaning, with every turn you make love will encircle your path of purpose.

Enjoy the adventure.

Signs are everywhere, in shapes, words, thoughts, mistakes, numbers, people . . .

Be vulnerable
Forgiveness
Perception
Courage
Imagine
Believe
Love
Risk
Fail
Fall
Be

Can you see through the words? Unlock the secrets as they reveal the truth. *Use your key.*

When you find your key, note you will be free to use your voice within.

Think before you speak, are your words clear and foremost positive? Are you sending a good message and more importantly living true to what you preach or in how you live?

Too many throw up words and do not clarify their meaning nor pronounce good intention.

Collect yourself until the moment when you have elevated your "Sacred Being" in living abundantly with your *whole heart*. This does not mean walk on pins and needles, it simply means care for what you are saying. You are in learning stages of vocabulary. Old sanes, jokes and thoughts, beliefs they do not add up anymore. Listen to them and see for yourself. In transforming your former self and modifying your vocabulary, you do need to think before you talk.

I had too, and I love what words means to me now, how they transcend to others. The compassion and truth my words speak. They are renewed with good intent and love, and yes, I still have a bittersweet sense of humor, only it does not cost in pain to others.

Times change, people change, and so do words. One thing that does not change is love, like a dog it remains loyal and full of *unconditional love*.

A fun and enlightening sign for me. Turn the word dog around and you *get* GOD—
Always there, walking with you. Same goes for words. Now some may think nothing changes, it makes no great enduring difference. It is a matter of perspective and *imagination*, a matter of everything love.

In Making One Think
Not
By Controlling His Mind
Only For The *Soul Purpose*
To Inspire
"A Better Today"

A few things that confront us in life. When we know deep down we must but cannot aloud or quite the opposite. Think of these tools and signs as a rope, grab on—in your mind, spirit, or physical self, climb them one at a time, as you need them. Build your endurance mentally so you may achieve the challenge of succeeding in your goals therefore maintaining good, in your life. You may be bound up emotionally. No worries. This is a practice and it needs your undivided attention. Approach it slowly or go at it firmly. You may find yourself at both ends at different times.

Remember there is no right or wrong way just simply your way.

As long as you are sincere and serious about change, you have nothing to worry about *except* that voice in your head. I think of him as a little man no bigger than my pinkie finger, whispering literally sweet nothings in my ear, creating doubt, fear, hate, anger, jealousy, sadness and so on. He knows you very well, he will trip you if you do not pay attention. And believe me, most the time when you have made a wrong move or spoke out of ill surely he was behind it! Take back your ear and focus; you need clarity. He will fall back when he knows you are on to him, he loses his power because you have learned how to manifest your skills. You have become conscious and aware. Taking full responsibility for your actions. Now you may pursue your dreams of passion.

You must love you, deep down in order to complete the cycle *"connecting mind, body, and soul."*

We attempt one or two steps and at different times in connecting these three compartments. Also some of us don't know that to support a healthy lifestyle, to have balance and stay on point one must be connected to their emotions. If you are one whom struggles with weight issues? Reach deep down and tune in, why? This goes for many other topics of emotion.

Come to understand your emotions; do not run or push them away. They will rebel against you trying to get your attention. Find out what they want. They are there for a reason.

Harmony in balance

Balance sometimes means jumping outside the circle; know the harmony is within you. Once you get the hang of your tune, you will play the melody, beautifully. You are energy not a robot. Sing and dance along to your rhythm. Be the music, that is how we hear it play, channel your authentic self. Sound waves connect us all and we love music for goodness sake we are plugged in, are we not?

You are an instrument—play, listen, enjoy.

To a degree, one must be in sync with Sacred Self to balance all human makeup. The way we work is more complex and it is up to us to be the Scientist, the Doctor, and the Artist. In being a doer you might find it easier. Whatever your personality may be without trying your very best you will not serve your future self well. Spite what you have heard you are the designer of your own life and you have choice. Make it count now. Time travels through past, present, and future. Rediscover your sacred self.

Some may be scholars, engineers, athletes, self-taught, if you hold certifications, licenses, master degrees. Wonderful for you! To achieve one's goal in education truly does open doors. Those of you without a simple GED but within you, hold the key. There is a plan instilled in you and then there is the master of purpose made for you, *go after it, set it free.* Do not be held back by ignorant thought that you are less than.

I promise you have something very important to offer, a wisdom, an idea, kind words, imagination, a message to unfold. You were made to be bold, creative, strong, kind, thoughtful . . . I can go on for days! Look in the mirror study yourself well. Pay no mind in what others have said about you or to you, listen for your voice, it has something to say. See within your true beauty. Study your books for they are there, study *nature* for it is also there, study love for it *is*.

A man who sets out for his own knowledge is a man whom will make his mark.

All of Life in a Metaphor

Material things in life except for the necessary items you will find are of no use to you on your journey.

You will come to need less and *feel* more, be assured there is comfort in knowing.
This change helps with useless distraction.

Material you will need of capacity are of the following:
A Rope, A Key, *and* Love.

"It is for you to find them."

By the time you are done reading this, you may understand or maybe you do now. Some may come to realize it later on. That is part of the fun in your adventure! I still enjoy the epiphanies and surprises. It keeps you wanting more of the good life within and essentially understanding what it means to cross over. Times, people, circumstances are always changing. There is not a master of knowing anything for certainty BUT you can and will come to "a knowing" of self and in that my love *is* freedom.

Without purpose, *what is the Point*? Ask yourself that.

As a matter of fact, I dare you to ask yourself many questions about you.
Things of value, importance, or just for fun! This journey is to be taken lightly *and* seriously, balance.

I believe it is the most exciting and extraordinary thing that has ever happened to me. I thank God for waking up for if I did not I would be dead or in a straitjacket. So rest assured, you are on a venture of a lifetime, if so choosing to walk this path.

"A wake in conscious thought and feeling all the love that is missing in the lives of people is most heartbreaking and torture for I love open and honestly from my heart and trust *in* God to lead me forth to help make a difference through living strong and faithfully, living the influence for the greater good of all."

In times, being honest with oneself can appear dishonest to another.

We need more depth to live in harmony. Some may need less, others more of.

Truth is; all of these words when read come alive and they are being shared with you, meant for you to find what works for you. You need to understand your *body, mind, and soul*—how it works, what it needs to grow.

In a simple truth; if you keep consuming more than you need in possessions for the acceptance of others in whom know no better than you. You will come to find those who rest on worldly things become obsessed in satisfying an empty hole inside in turn selling themselves cheap or too high in standard. To imprison oneself in a house rather than a home. Too exist in a dull and passionless life safely to only find yourself anxiety ridden and depressed wishing for a better tomorrow and subjecting yourself to a tomb of negative and hateful aggression, growing toxicity inside your very Soul. You will be that tragic story always yearning and searching for more to complete you. You will never be content or feel gracious because you have spited all that is true, *for what?*

I know this very well, no matter how much money I had, how pretty I would make myself, the love I shared with another. Truth was I still felt empty and left needing more. Until I faced my truth and started loving me and dated myself . . . *yes,* I dated me for a time and *loved it.* Till this very day in writing this book I am expanding my drive willing the truth and daring to love in a way I had never dreamed I could do out loud. I pondered and appreciated others who lived content, in this way of living.

"Love is inside of you and all you need is to recognize your presence."

You never know when life will bring turmoil but with no thought. I embrace my faith *in* God and by doing just that, I trust myself more. So I face the trouble head on and go through it. *It is life not forever.* I am coming to know my Sacred Self and she is timeless, talented, eternally grateful, wise to know—heaven is at her footstep. So I will continue to follow the rainbow spite the turmoil, the stars will light up every night, as the sun amazingly shines its warmth down on me and lights the path that runs through the river in which connects all that is right in the world. It promises to keep me warm when it is cold, and when I cold, my heart *is always* warm.

"For I am Peace, For I am Love, For I Am."

Divinity in Healing

I remember the very moment I knew I had to count on myself for it was a choice I made, and I have honored it since. From making this promise to count on myself, it has taught me things of great measure. Learning to *feel,* to *understand* how my body works. When my health failed once again and there were no better solutions for me at the time amongst society. I took it upon myself at my most desperate hour in need, tired of the pain and suffering for too many years, interfering with my life no more.

I took action and on my knees crying out to God asking for a healing, a miracle, a sign!

I cannot burden others with what it is I need to be or feel complete. Just because someone is qualified, certified, licensed, having the right credentials does not make them immortal nor better than. Even in matters of the heart.

I had a calling and I had a *responsibility* to heal with Divinity through contacting my sacred self with exercises and practice. With the help of my doctors, mentors, friends, and family. It was time for me to go inside and find yet another healing or discovery. Others no longer could provide what I needed to undergo personally. I would soon learn more about love, healing of my spirit and truth, with God beside me.

To give genuine quality care, for in doing so we receive tranquility *in* peace.
May we then be given a divine sense of healing and hope.

We all have a duty and it is up to each individual to specialize in the quality of work they perform. I alone found that to blame another person was society telling me what to do and how to think, and that little pinkie size of a man whispering in my ear. I would put an end to all negative intel.

Trusting in

Imagination would accompany me on this journey.
I would walk away from everything and everyone
God and his angels, along with my chosen guides, would be my confidants
I had to trust *in*
Not contacting my friends and family
Would be beneficial to my healing and growth.
I would not be forever gone but for a moment away
In time they would come to understand
For I would improve and grow fluent in the language of love
For the better understanding and soon healing of all men

Shining a white coat of heaven smelling of sweet roses
God promised me if I would *trust in* a divine process all would be right
I trust in him so away I went.

Live in your imagination and find freedom in your beautiful state of mind with love guiding you.

"Colors are ever so beautiful and multidimensional.
The sky is infinite with wonder and sur-
prises coming from the North.
Dragonflies and butterflies are everywhere and they circle me
as if they are giving me their blessing. Nature is splendid and
comforting I do not fear the coming of the storm for it warns
the fools who do not believe and for me I find comfort in the
rain, the wind as it brushes through my hair. The trees stand tall
like soldiers protecting the souls who find shelter under their
shields of silky coated leaves. Their branches are like arms and
hands to catch the falling trenches of evil and dark spells that
those who know no better cast with ill intentions and fear. Lost
is no one who sees the land as a home, food is plentiful and the
life that lives in the soil working all day and everyday on mak-
ing right with the light. I am of the light and I will continue to
make room by bettering myself and loving myself understand-
ing the good that awakens my Soul each and every new day. I
open my eyes and listen to what God is telling me. I feel with
all that I am, I am light. I am the land that they may step upon
to reach the ponds to drink from its nectar in the earth. So
care for me so I can care for you is what I hear in my heart, it
is what sets me apart from the criminals who steal nothing and
lose everything. Be of gold and bathe in the riches of Love."

Happiness
is yours.
Seek and you shall find
Thy love within
is exquisite
Be still in the patience of silence,
For there will be people
who come into our lives for a time
like a season
Let them add to your happiness
nay to condemn them to a harsh loyalty
Love them freely
place no blame when it tis over
Enjoy thy moment
not in time spent
For time is of essence
A moment ever enchanting
in our hearts forever
Growing like seeds in heaven's garden.

Take responsibility for your needs, and if you are pure of heart
in your attempt, you will find the very reasons why things happen—
in the *good* and in the *bad*. A time will come when it will eventually
have you seeking truth in your life, like I did and continue too. In
my life's work if it being a clerk, bartender, hairdresser, babysitter,
life coach, personal trainer, even when I cleaned houses I gave my
very best! *"There is no small job only is there a small mind of thinking."*
The important truth is I do everything with all my heart and give
my full undivided attention to each and every person I come in
contact with. Quality, vision, action, and conscious thought. It has
never been about the money for me. *"I do what it is I love and I love
people."* A humble servant is true.

I am not what I do, but in essence, of who I am.

Passion, it excites me, it thrills me, *it is all that I am*—all in or not at all!

I love me, myself, and I, as I should because it took me a long time to appreciate who I am. God created me and you, for that we are blessed so I feel gratified and want what is best for all souls alike.

I found God in search of my sanity.

I was raised to *treat others as you want to be treated*.

Now not to say I have always at every second been clear and had the best of intention, I have fallen weak to insecurities and ignorance, I am only human people! But majority of the time I have had and still have good friends, acquaintances and loved ones whom I know would vouch for me. I always have the best of intentions.

I am a flower in bloom and change of season grows me to live in harmony with the gardens of love.

"I am hard at times but always for good reason.
My heart is pure and open but still I carry my sword for no man ever disrespects another for if this shall pass my sword will cross his heart."

We are easy to fall prey to those who are eager for their own mass of desire. Especially when kindness is present for evil preys on those whom are meek in their way. Stand tall and sure. Be heartfelt and love for it will be your shield of armor against a dark heart.

Desire fades *as you find* True Passion
Nothing can replace the magnetic pull of complete pleasure ongoing
Cautious for Desire will leave you bitter and empty
Sex and money are the toys of men and women
The Dark one veil over you distraction of will
"Honesty is the price"
A debt you will be responsible for paying in consequence
For if you sell yourself in skin, change will be thrown at you

On your knees, you will come to beg forgive-
ness, leaving you naked on the stone
Where you gave yourself away for free
Charity your penalty
For who are you but the sex you gave them for profit in neglect
Respect yourself for you are beautiful and strong
Love is your name"

"When I channel patience with the love of nature pure of intention I can swim forever in glory of man."

Noise, confusion, sex, illusion
Find a space where you can meditate
Free fall and die.
Be reborn in silence and calm, passion, imagination
Be *in a love state* of mind

"Be true in your identity."

I could not depend on others to help or save me they could only do so much it was time for me to give up and give in.

A few steps that will bring you to everlasting change.

1. Breaking point: nothing more to lose, or you have lost everything and everyone. Giving in finally, desperation.
2. Becoming vulnerable: letting go, free fall.
3. Wanting: the good life, love and all that you are deserving of, begin to seek.
4. Needing: sick of having nothing, your heart is aching for a deeper connection, healing, forgiveness.
5. Illness: the need, want, and importance to be healthy.
6. Epiphany: a sudden knowing, it is simply your time, inspiration.
7. A Calling: a sense you are meant for something greater, it is time to fulfill your purpose.

Some will ignore the nudging of change, there are people who thought me crazy and mad, saying she will never be happy and does not know what she wants. That I was a gypsy. For maybe at times, I am a gypsy, a hippie, for I am honored by the spirit to live free. I am not one thing but many. Like a lion, I am fierce and brave and like an angel, I love and pray for all to have peace and know joy. It is not in who we portray but the love that resides in are heart, the warmth in our soul—are truth, the wisdom and tune we hold dear in our mind and how it shows toward others.

Maybe they were just afraid to lose me. No one person can ever be lost when there is love present. Few do understand my truth for the choices I have made and continue to. Most do love me and believe in me, if they agree with my decisions or not. It is my belief some are meant to stand still, and others driven to create the change that evolves all of us.

For those whom deny their chosen path they will only suffer and find themselves in déjà vu, panic, and self-destruction mode. I ignored these déjà vus thinking not much of them, amused if anything. Thinking it was my imagination, fighting it because to be honest playing on the dark side was tempting, easy and until I was ready. I would begin to play and learn from the dark and gain knowledge to take back with me so I may enlighten others to follow in the light. I was so glad when I finally gave in to my calling entirely, sad for I would move on from loved ones once again.

I began to strength train my will and fill my heart with love. Focused in on seeking the light. I now was in control of my life and not being subject to drama and consequence from meaningless desires and false role models. I made a choice, the right one for me and I am so happy I did. It has made a world of positive difference in my life and those I love. Making a peace with my past, present, and future.

Trust me when I say I was that girl who believed that black cloud was for me, I laugh now when I think about it. Pay attention to your surroundings, look for signs they are everywhere. Do not go mad by this, just be present and willing. Believing will come in the process of change. Do never be burdened by those you leave behind. Trust me no one gets left behind who shares in love and truth from their heart.

Be patient and give in to your calling it only wants you to know how wonderful you are and to remind you, all you have to offer. Please know you are not crazy for being different than your family or other mates. Search for your truth. Be brave in your difference.

I am different, *and* different is *wonderful*.

In my desperation, he was there. *God*.

He goes by many names and wherever you find him
In whatever name you choose to call him by.
He is there
I do not judge man for his religion, color, cul-
ture, sacrifice, nor beliefs
Therefore, I do choose
to stand on the side of truth, where good resides.
There is no side divided
except for those who have become bitter and blinded by darkness
for every man who still pays a heavy price of burden.
I pray for you
In God's hands, I place my confusion and receive grace.

Holy Judgment

Should we promise to renew ourselves once a week through remembering what is Holy and what is good for love is bringing us home.

I love thy neighbor as my own but my trust I place in the hands of GOD.
In this I have peace, always.

And as they continued to ask him, he stood up and said to them, "Let him who is without sin among you be the first to throw a stone at her." (John 8:7, English Standard Version)

For I saw Jesus in her smile and loved her more.

"No man or woman, even child, animals and aliens, plants and the wild—be kind for who knows what truly is. Nothing is as it seems. Hear things one way and later you shall see it differently. "Be Love" for it is our only truth. Everything else is a lesson lived or a test failed. Love and you will be forever pleased, happy and well."

Smiling, laughing, and *loving* **is** a universal language.
For the day will come where we all will know the language of love.

To say you're sorry and truly mean it. To accept an apology with open arms. These two forms of forgiveness take inner strength and humbleness. It is not easy but when all's said and done there is freedom and incredible merciful flow that runs through your entire body creating instant happiness. One may even experience tears of joy. I have felt this love and it is worth all it takes in strength.

"Through having my Spirit broken it is only then did my Soul emerge from my lifeless body. Driven now to make all things I have within me, right."

How I Have Come To Know Peace through Forgiveness:

I needed to forgive those whom have hurt me. I speak in the present, being that even when you have aligned yourself with truth. Our lives are ever moving and connecting to another. When we succeed in efforts and come to peace with emotions we are changing once again. This journey is compartmental. It has taken time, effort and falling down to stand up taller than before. I did not suddenly just forgive. On my journey, I learned how to forgive. I found through experience that people most the time are not intent on hurting us but living their lives not better nor worse than us. I had to walk in their shoes to understand I was someone too that has caused hurt to others. I was aware now of my faults and actions. Compassion found me at a time of sadness and angst.

I am in constant awe of its power so it empowers me to become more love and ever so forgiving of all whom have had some part in my life good, bad and the ugly. Again, this is a very important topic and there is much to tell. But this read is not meant to divulge everything. Just peek previews, thoughts and poetry to set you on an adventure with love being your Spirit Guide.

A test maybe to see if you are worthy of such a divine privilege. I myself, hate tests and fall under their pressure but I am learning how to focus and be in control, find a calm and composure in understanding. I will not allow fear to rule over my life any longer, so I choose to be brave and face diversity!

The choice is always ours. We are not given many choices in this world we live yet on this road trust me choice is yours.

Finding confidence through building inner peace.

Question: If you were suddenly aware of your negative behaviors and saw they were influencing your loved ones, would you attempt to change for the better?

And yet another change is upon
All excepting
I am
One of the stages is not quite fun
all too exhausting,
Truth is
Been here many times before
Just is
getting used to the idea
of relaxing, being in the moment
—Just me.

> *"Fear does not have to be anything but a word; we give it life.*
> *Quit fear. It's just a bad habit that gets more atten-*
> *tion than it should, like a fad.*
> *Focus on positive adrenaline running through your blood.*
> *Stimulate your every waking state of mind!*
> *Inspirit the light that moves your soul."*

Rino, my youngest
Photo taken by Shanna

The photo was inspired by all the love I hold within my heart to share because there is always more love to go round.

To Look Up To Someone Else for Love of Self

In doing this you expose yourself to heartbreak with major symptoms leading to bitter choices, the coldness will set in and hateful anger will begin to breed. In one's horrific state, a low self worth mistaking true kindness and you will believe love to be deceitful and worse untrue.

There true love masked as one we do not think could be, so this love we pass evidently.

For I, too, once passed through, I looked up to others to satisfy my cravings, thinking there was one person whom can complete me. I always left broke and longing for more desire and almost died from the emptiness and loneliness that spread through. I was weak and alone again and again until one fine day I woke upon a beautiful truth realizing I was, *"the One."* I had all the love I needed and I became full in richness with infinite being. "In *needing less, and loving more."*

When one is abandoned, they are left without hope, or love of self maybe love of self begins at home. So when we are abused, left or simply ignored by those we look up to, we are left with a hole in our heart. And we fill it with neglectful thoughts, shame, disappointment, and a bitter sadness that feeds on emptiness. What they don't know "the abandoned" is they are special individuals that are not being punished yet have within them a strength, a unique and admirable will—to defeat the very cause of what is wrong and they have within them to make all things right.

These people among the abandoned by their loved ones have a charisma, a charm. A confident and vulnerable love about them. They are loved by many yet feel loved by no one. If they only knew that it was not what they did wrong and they were not left but merely empowered to help the world and were given up to be more for a much bigger plan than what they could ever expect.

Those with mighty thoughts have a greater ability to aspire a break in the wrong behaviors. Who will dare stand up to fate and rule over this planet with love . . .

"In a truth we are all abandon in nature to find ourselves in true love by one another."

For no man is lost without his heart, as his guide. So if you allow your heart to love more and in broader terms, you will not ever be lost only saved, carried, and made to be a warrior of love. So be the Soul to teach the children to appreciate what they have and not come to count on Ego as their confidant. For if you are meant to have it, it will certainly would be.

I may be late . . .
yet I am always on time.

Trust synchronicity for it will lead you home.

Moral is

We can cry the blues for the cruelty put on to us or we can stand up and make a truce with the hurt and *lead* with all our might for may we be soldiers of love and deny hate for it has no more power to destroy. I pray for you my friend for I have been there, loved there and now choose to make room for the light, within you.

You have possibility within you . . .
You have Love inside of you
Make room for the light *and* all will be right.

Love Is the Coolest Thing on the Planet

It holds sacred divine purpose to share in its richness and pleasure.

Do not forget your heart workout for the day
"Be love"
Connecting mind, body, and soul

Photo taken by Shanna on a nature walk.

Amazed by the faithful message God portrays through nature. Take the time to truly explore and be touched as I.

Remember your heart needs tending to. It is a muscle that holds endless capacity for the treasures we keep, hold them dear. Workout all that pain and forgive, strength training your heart is essential to good health. This heart of yours has many secrets to care and pumps for heart pounding flutters—that *awesome crazy feeling love has about it!* So throw a heart warm up in with that set of bicep curls and you tread master heroes!

Soul Food

May love be present in life, our health depends on it. In the food we eat and the beverage we choose. Feed your body well, it is important and detrimental on your passage. Satisfy your sweet tooth with pure sugar cane, *natural.* Balance in everything, don't punish yourself, treat yourself.

No need to substitute what is already of the land, made for you and for me.

Be nutritious and enjoy your food. Trust in how it makes you feel, know where it comes from and how it is cared for . . .

The care that goes into making one's food is the love that will provide you with a deeper sense of being and strength. *It is our responsibility to care.*

In supplements, do the research, there are herbs to heal, made from the land. Do your homework, maybe replace your scripts for natural remedies, they are there for you. Create balance.

Meditation: learn it, and take part in it, again. You knew of it before you joined the world. For water in its purest form, blends well with any fruit, infuse your beverages with passion. Alcohol is **not** therapy, it will mask as your friend, you know better. Enjoy it on occasion but do not abuse it for it will be gone from your lips forever. Be safe and love yourself well. Your actions will have consequences be in the moment true. For your body is your vessel—cherish it, maintain it, love it. *Bon Appetit!!*

Eat to live and be merry, *live not* to eat and drown in the drink.

For it is not the weight you carry in fat nor age, long worn skin, it is in the heavy burden of ill—emotional constipation if you will!

To replace real food with chemicals is ludicrous!
It is not in the fat, but in the ingredients . . .

Why Fitness Is Essential

Fitness is very important to me not because of vanity, though *"It is okay to want to look good!"* In looking good I have found I feel good. I will not lie. I am a visual person so, I do like to look present-able. I am in the beauty biz for over twenty years, so you can say I have an eye for quality. I appreciate beauty, as wellness. I love fashion and have a flair for color! I also am in touch with another side of myself who is more present today. A free spirit lives within me and I let her out more these days. I am learning how to appreciate my flaws, this takes practice! For I am comfortable in my own skin for beauty is in the eye of the beholder. Not quite understanding what that meant years ago? Through evolving my consciousness, as a life coach and individual, I feel I do now understand. We need to focus the view from within **not** *only outward.*

"I feel my best when I am in my own skin."

What that means for me is, when I am in balance with mind, body, and soul.

Getting back to fitness, working out gives positive returns always, when you do it right. *Invest in you,* with someone who cares and is passionate. It is not about the money. This responsibility is on you. You would not leave your children with just anyone so put yourself with a trainer, specialist who will invest in you, just the same. If you need recommendations, I will be happy in referring you in the right direction, you just need ask.

Positive energy and results from working out or simply being active.

- It gives back the good stuff we need.

I am a high-energy person and working out or being active helps me with creating a happier mood.

- It stimulates good ideas and motivation.

I have more confidence to face life and challenges.
- I am open to love more freely.

Obstacles now are more like amusement, and my fierce Lion comes out to tackle every time!
I feel like I can conquer the world, do anything when I work my body.

A few movements I enjoy. Find one that fits you. There are plenty of activities to choose from.

- Yoga
- Weight training
- Stretching
- Meditative practice(meditation)
- Walking
- Dancing
- Breathing exercises
- Swimming

In "connecting mind, body, and soul" you find yourself in a happier state of being. I no longer feel fatigue or depression that comes with being idle for too long. We are energy so it makes sense we have to keep our bodies moving, right?! For me, personally, I have learned to channel my unsettled energy and form a positive connection through working out and staying fit.

What works for one may not work for another but do know if you do not move your body, your body will begin to break down and affect others areas of wellness and therefore your health will be at risk.

It is your responsibility to care for yourself and being thought conscious and mindful.

In creating love vibes, you have the ability to be anything you want!

Don't be eluded by size or color. The attitude of a person is what counts. Confidence radiates love. People will be inspired and affected by the energy you portray.

I choose to believe in the best of myself and inspire others to be the best within themselves.

Creating positive influence wear.

Nobody is the same, no being alike for you are made in love, unique and different do not look to another for what you should ambulate in size nor beauty for "you are you" and to someone, appreciated and adored more than you know.

For those
who cannot physically
move within their bodies
or breathe in a natural way
You have a heart, use it.
"Be love"
Be in a state and meditate.
Meditation is a practice
all of us can do
with love.
If you are present
there is always
a way

to be the very best
you have
within you.

Be comfortable in your own skin. *Are you*? Are you looking at others wishing that it was you? Let me stop you for a minute because in my experience I have seen with my own eyes and heard with my own ears.

An earlier experience of mine, I was a hairdresser and I had a prom party of girls and each one looking at the other mumbling how they wanted her hair and how the other whispering the same wish or loving the blue in her eyes better than her own.

Witnessing this in a moment I wanted to make them all aware for each of their beauty, rare and adored by the other. We make too much emphasis on what we see in magazines and television. It was not till I worked in photography did I see the truth and discover the Photoshop editing that was being made to disillusion the truth in the beauty of the person being photographed. I had my photo done and the photographer erased my so-called flaws and personally I looked fake. I had to really look and study myself to see the true beauty and it had been erased.

I am thankful for that experience for I now know the truth. I can definitely see how we get confused but please know that your flaws are your trademarks. The hidden beauty is inside. Be creative with your vanity but do not substitute or trade in your secrets. Too many are sabotaging themselves and their loved ones with lies. Be faithful to what is real and beautiful, it is the rarity in difference that beauty resides.

Beauty is in the eye of the beholder.

—*Molly Brawn*, novel by
Margaret Wolfe Hungerford

To enhance a photo is one thing to camouflage it is another.

Why was I the only one witnessing the very obvious of stares I will tell you true because insecurity blinded them? A sense of neglect in confidence, a society telling us what to wear, manipulating what truly was there. Taking the magazine's fashion and entertainment as the daily word. For when we look into the mirror and love ourselves even have mere confidence in something good in ourselves is beyond compare.

"Appreciate beauty of thy neighbor never be jealous and so cynical in comparison, each masterpiece is artistically imperfect, upon love is beauty."

Feed your soul with compliments
ask of no one to tell their thoughts, their view, opinions of you
The very cost of your worth will be perse-
cuted, know yourself to be true.
We must ask that of ourselves.
Know you are beautiful, handsome
made just right in the eyes of the beholder.
Work out your heart for it is love, that **is**.
Drink from thirst in purity.
Smile at everything and everyone
this will leave a positive trace,
like breadcrumbs left for others to eat and to sew.
Brand not in the labels that you wear but in the love and warmth
in the strength that you endure and share
In your will **stand** for courage
Trust in all your beauty, for it is rare.
beautifully you!

Anger

Aggressive behavior from being too much hurt, sad, or disappointed.

It also ignites emotions to stir from the shame, insecurity and weakness buried deep down.

Sometimes it is easier to be mad but like all prescription drugs, it also can be highly addictive and before you know it, you are hooked, and before long, your emotions are not your own but dark and dismal, taking on a false sense of self. You may come to find comfort in this state but I promise you, it is not worth the great loss, it will drive you mad. Instead, become in control of your anger, channel your frantic energy, take back your life, and derive a difference being better than you once were, be a leader in a mass of dark followers. Draw from the light within you be a warrior not its victim. Make something out of that which has caused you such misery and dread.

You are not alone in this war. There are others, I am one of them. I have fought many times and a survivor I have chosen to be. A warrior being who has found peace in knowing I have it in me to create endless amounts of invention and have distributed throughout my life. I have reinvented myself many times and only stronger I am for it. The darkness now is my keynote to helping others heal and find true happiness that lives. It is why I will lead and not choose to walk behind the line of evil desire.

Which road do you choose?

As you have heard before I am quite sure of it, *"Rough times make the man"* (Unknown).

Who do you choose to do be? A survivor or a victim?

I chose to be a survivor and came out of all my diversity, *a warrior!*

We make for uncomfortable times so we may move forward to where we are needed. We are each other's teacher, student and guide, "HOPE for the future." Healing for the moment and yes—the moment is now.

Be the change you want to see in the world.

— Ghandi

The subconscious mind is far from one with the conscious mind, "awake" to truth no longer will you be ignored or in the dark.

Pain is complex in a world that is suffering from sleepy souls. Wake up and stop thinking *that black cloud is for you* or that you are not worthy of having a good life. You are one who has this amazing energy core growing inside of you.

A blue print. Put the pieces together and build your life up and right. And if you don't get it the first time *start over again.* Time is of the essence and on your side when you are in motion with the Divine purpose in store for you, your very purpose.

Definition of core; the central, innermost
The very most essential part of anything.
Also known as a **magnetic core**.
It is energy, electric, *electricity.*

There are no right or wrong ways just bad behavioral habits and as all habits go **they can be broken**. Explore the possibility, the grand gesture, the winning numbers, the true love you are waiting for. It is not in your head you are not crazy and the dreamer in you is being born as you read this right now . . .

How do you feel? To know in your heart what is real, possible and meant for you.

So now unplug what you have learned, heard, been told, not told and like an infant take a new breath, open your eyes and look at life again with a new perspective. Even dare to play!

The most wonderful and awkward reality is to learn how to play again and not thought of as crazy, weird or indifferent.

Take care of your mind,
in developing a cure for thinking is the time, lost you will not be.

Love Truth 101

In my experience for example, when a child learns how to read and write for the first time, or when someone who is having physical therapy learning how to walk again. You literally don't have to make excuses, like for instance, one must have a nephew or a child in witness to or simply enjoy a toy store! It is an odd feeling I still look over my shoulder, is anyone looking, what will they think!? Are you serious really? LOL, come on, this is so silly, I keep teaching myself how to think like a kid and it takes much practice. It is a mindset, a new horizon of thought conscious motion, just be in your moment, don't think *just be.*

It is working for me and I will be playing in full fun in no time at all! Have fun, kids, growing back down and reaching higher than you ever could imagine, be childlike in your demeanor and grown up like a strong maple humbled and delighted to meet anyone who appreciates her limber. I believe it is the children who are the teachers and we the students. Do *not* hush them play with them, listen, and be.

An adult becomes old in their spirit when they go into hiding stay within the youth in loving with all your heart, <u>feel</u> the pain and <u>continue</u> on to an <u>understanding</u>.

We still think we cannot do much to better the world, I am here to tell you the good news! YES, one person, it starts with one person to make a positive connection, *change.* Stand out and *be!*

You want love, be love. you want peace, be peace, you want truth, tell it!

Inspire the very things you want from others. Lead by living a positive and true experience. For us to connect together in and not divided from.

Social media has proven people follow people, it is in the numbers even the paid for numbers! If you think about it we invite strangers into our lives daily. "Unintentional connection" We follow each other, like and share. In truth, **you are that one person to change the world for the better,** in thy own realm of belief the secret to world peace we all have had in us all along. Love yourself, *forgive*, be free from what has changed you for the worse. You are not your circumstance; no child is their parent. You are a rare and powerful gem plug in to your magnificence and be the first so others will be inspired, enlightened to stand with you. He who stalks may not be so much a threat but a friend who only feels closer to fellow man.

In being vulnerable, be mindful in sense.

Journaling and Scrapbooking

This would be the time to start a journal or begin again. You don't have to be a great writer to have a journal or even spell very good for that matter. Just doodle, try your best. Use pictures from magazines. A kind of scrapbook, it is yours to create however you like as long as it works for you. It is important to speak of what hurts you, pains you, fears you, angers you, saddens you. Even your happy times, goals you may have, dreams . . . *Write them down!*

We must be able to confide our secrets if not we repress them and that is no good for us or for others around us. If you are like me and never want your journal found and read aloud by someone other than you, we have all heard those stories! Well, do a ritual burn.

A ritual burn is my way of writing down my most intimate thoughts, reading them aloud, processing what I wrote and why, then I say a prayer short and brief and burn it—in a safe manner, of course.

It leaves me feeling content and at ease, refreshed and ready to move on. It is sacred to me and it has helped me achieve my goals, except love for the beauty of it. Let go, forgive. Sometimes I even get really crafty and set an unrealistic goal write it down and read it weeks, months, years later and guess what? It came true!

There is a magic about your journal you give it life, the love and honesty you trust in it to protect your secrets. This is what it is for me. I believe in God, and even when I am in doubt, he reveals signs and I simply follow those signs and one led me to my journal of faithful magic.

I never liked and even rebelled against journals thinking them as just something everybody else did. Not being one to follow the crowd I thought, not me. I was wrong when God showed me what to do; I went about it my own special way.

I am thankful for the journal and for God in showing me the way.

Recently I just started a Live Journal on the web and it helped carry me out of a dark time. I fell ill again winter of 2015 and I began to fall into a depression I was already struggling with anxiety from my health related issues. I needed to do something ASAP! Knowing too well what would happen if I didn't choose to help myself and again seek out guidance.

"Being vulnerable in a world of judgment set me free in a way that has captivated my movy—my motivation!"

A Fun Quiz Dare

1. Do you believe in yourself?(circle the answer of choice)
    Yes or No

2. Why?

3. What is the hardest thing you have ever had to overcome?

4. Who inspires you?

5. What do you do for a living?

6. *Does it give you purpose?*   Yes or No

7. *Are you moving or standing still?*

8. *When you were a child who was it you aspired to be?*

9. Are you young as or older than?(are you young at heart)

10. Do you feel if you laid your head down tonight and passed on, would you feel it was worth it all *or would you wish you did something different?*   Yes or No

11. Are you living the way you want, the way you are told or perhaps you never really thought about it?

12. Rate your level of happiness from 1 to 10.

13. *What is your most favorite quality in yourself—you would want someone to notice yet never would say or admit aloud?*

14. *How often do you lie to yourself and your loved ones?*

15. Finally, are you proud of the life you live?   Yes or No

16. Do you workout or stay active?   Yes or No
    What is stopping you if your answer is no?

"Be Love"

Control not love for it is free
Choke it not with unkind words
For I cannot die, *said love*
Poison my food but not my love for you
Your behavior is toxic yet your heart broken
from things like sadness, disappointment and hurt?
Let me mend your spirit
For my love **is** free
I give it to you without condition—no payment is necessary
Your Soul, starving
Allow me to awaken you with seeds of love
For if you bend the words, I love you, to your will
Tainted with fear you instill
Let go, let go, let go
Kill this toxic ego
Filled with lies and manipulation
Breathe in, let the light in
Breathe in, let me, love in
Bitter is the sadness in your soul
Free yourself how I love you
Blame no one nor you
Invite love—the door is open
Be not disappointed
Look into the mirror and know I love you so
It is I—

CHAPTER 3

Term

Transfer of Energy Relaxation Meditation

"Meditation is strength training for the mind, body and soul. Many of us lose our spirits as life and loved ones come along and change everything as we know it."

I believe it is where God resides—within us.

A Poem of Prayer

Grant me the strength, dear Lord,

To not give up to keep climbing, to not fall victim to the dark ones lure and evil whispers but to be lifted by you and your angels. Send me mine today at this very moment. My heart may it be open to your will for I then will know peace. Help me to forgive myself, you, and for those whom have hurt and disappointed me.

To not be led by empty desires, fall weak and act in harmful behavior. Help me to stand tall and step away from anything or anyone that does not have good intention.

Dearest God,

If I may ask you to be present in my life and even if I do not believe just yet still be here until I do and further may I be present in myself to speak, hear or see only love from this moment on.

Amen,

Thank you,
Lord

"Meditation connects us with our true natural state of being."

Transforming our conscious thoughts through to a magical energy as it sails us to a realm from gravity's pull.

Let go of negative thoughts, hateful feelings, abandon all sense of worthlessness.

What you may be going through in suffering, know it is not forever but simply for now.

When we fight anything, we are showing resistance. Practice oneness with self and gel into a true state of being. All will be right with truth. Do not be afraid for it may be uncomfortable, it may sting but do know life will be good within.

Be a warrior and make room for the light—*your light.*

Coming to TERM sends us and releases us to a place where we are magical, our light is able to shine brighter. No gravity is present, our bodies are weightless. We are of pure intention, perfect stillness and yet we are flexible in nature. Whatever we need, the answers and guidance are there rather to heal us, help us with everything and anything. If it is to focus, receive clarity, to strengthen, even teach us to let go and free fall.

"To transcend is to free fall from physical attachment through spirit of mind and love in, soul splendor."

TERM (Transfer of Energy Relaxation Meditation) is a state of being. A prayer state if you will. A safe place to visit, in reconnecting to sacred self, source, the universe. To connect with loved ones whom have moved on. A place, I call home. One can find answers here, to communicate with our subconscious mind, transform unto our true being.

Meditation in TERM is a higher elevation, in spirit.

In my meditation sessions I am one with the universe and all that is.

I am truth in all that comes through me during the session. Love is and always has my heart beating faster as it vibrates authentic self; at this time, the body is lifting, and sacred self is transcending inward exciting my very genuine moment. Shifting my mind to a focal point, my soul is now in transit of true being.

Meditation: It is a practice of love. Our own channel where we are beautiful, timeless, intelligent, strong, funny, tall, witty, clever—whatever you need. Think of it as a reboot, sometimes as a battery needs a charge, well we need something too. If it is a charge, a rest, a skill. Meditation is there for you and for me to collect whatever it is we need to serve and experience a better life here. Put yourself first so you may lend yourself in the right manner and give love unconditionally without exhausting our resources and loved ones.

It tis ever changing as we are yet remaining the same in essence-

"When in truth are we infinite in possibility."

I am proud of my past and reflect often by seeing it true. I believe it has helped in keeping my mind clear and my Soul content, happy and healthy. We all have one, to not look back is to not face the things that need attention, this truth will creep up and form a disease later in life.

Meditation is infinite in change and exquisite in love, to define it is to experience it within.

"Be Love"
Breathe in love
Breathe out love
In through your heart
Open your heart cavity
Ever expanding love
Let it in—
Another and another
Breathe in love, breathe out love
"Be love"

Finding yourself in a meditative state of healing, thinking, *feeling*.

It is not a foreign or new concept. I came upon it from my travels through Goodreads, conversations, with individuals whom have taken part, in their own lives. When I attempted meditation on my own—practicing and perfecting it, I learned how to apply the process of meditative state unto myself. I believe I was about thirteen years when I was playing with some spiritual activities, with some girlfriends at our weekly slumber party.

I was a natural, this is the time I found I had a gift as a medium. In a trance were my best friend had put me under and I easily drifted to the place, awaking scared out of my mind and swearing that I was a pregnant woman buried alive! It took an hour to calm me down. The girls were in quite a panic as well. Remember this was just a game, or was it? That next day is when I began practicing light as a feather, and it opened my eyes to another world entirely. I knew now there was more to this life. I was going to apply my gift and one day help people whom found themselves lost.

We all have it in us, to heal, learn, and create from within. Taking the skills and wisdom we have come across on our journey. It is not in the everyday items suggested to us.

That is how I came to write this book. From falling ill when a sickness visited me once again to help me slow down and do what it was I needed to do. In my healing process, I started to think seriously about writing a book. I have been told I should by people I know and adore. I loved writing and drawing as a child. I even wrote a short book and made it myself from scratch I was probably as young as seven years. I found it going through all of my writing materials, I guess it was destined. I forgot or maybe I thought it was too much out of my league.

Narrow minded thinking on my part. A meditative state of being gave me peace in seeing my life course there it was in my things to do, *write a book!* A close relative of mine was the final confidence piece I needed, write a book, she said. With all your positive influence and inspiration, you have a voice, Shanna, *use it!* There It was all the of the people whom have said something of that nature came rushing in, including a client, a dear friend whom told me years ago to write a book. I had no idea where to begin I had started a few times and got so lost and frustrated, I put it down.

Upon one day when the time was right, I in a state of being started writing a book not for any other reason but to serve my purpose and express my passion for love, truth and life. I have to say, a healing has again, come over me, seeing things differently. Passing through on memories has renewed something in me.

From writing truths, I have had no choice but to encounter ghosts, defining moments and words formed in another sense of discovering who I have become and yet remembering that girl I kind of forgot . . . The most important thing is; *I accomplished something I did not truly think I could.* Days away from completion and I am proud of my life, tears rolling down my face as I write the very last of words for you to read, and *I feel . . . thankful.*

If I could in some magical way, have you feel what this moment is bringing me . . . I would give it to you gracefully. I will not place my fears in the idea if this book is worthy or not to others. Truth is, it is making a positive difference in my life, and hopefully, it will bring peaceful bliss in the life of one person.

A personal prayer I have with God

This time was different. Though I prayed on it as I always do when I want and need to do something scary, big or outside my comfort zone.

I just had to say the words out loud . . . So I closed my eyes and began to pray.

GOD, I need you, please help me, guide me, work through me. Enlighten in me what is doubtful, show me what to do.

Thank you, God

"Staying God connected and staying true to myself is how I accomplish and maintain my goals."

In movement we find endurance.
In stillness we find wisdom.
In love we find happiness.
In truth we find peace.
therefore within.

The Value in Time

Finding balance in our life is not always easy and they sure did not teach it in my school growing up. I had to figure it out through experience in love, loss and in all the error of being human.

Time management: to value one's time, *boy there is money in that!* I didn't learn that—my time is of value till later on only after I had become a CHLC and the friendly advice of a friend. Know thy self to be true inspired by the William Shakespeare's famous quote; "to thine own self be true" *Hamlet*, 1.3.78

I gave myself away. It is a genetic trait, my father is the most generous man I know. He is very talented and intelligent but he gives himself away, giving himself little credit. He is deserving of more than he leads up to. Sadly society only respects those who charge a great price. I believe he is neglecting self-love, to know he is worth all the weight in gold. Raised with pure love intention, in honesty and humility. *To be honest,* I would not want him any other way. This has taught me well and I have learned how to achieve my goals from having the right love instilled in me. Morals, values, the essentials.

For I am blessed, all that I did have as a child. I never felt anything was missing in my life. So that I yearned for more love and adventure excited for what was and all there could be. Going back to time management, the day I realized my time is precious and because of my gift that I have come to embrace fully. It was dear that I take care of myself health wise, my energy is sacred and I need to be still and use it wisely.

"Be generous with your spirit yet mindful with your time."

My intent is to always help one in need. But I have to be mindful, for I am in God's hands and need to listen carefully to the very thing he wants for me and others who I have part in helping.

For all the times I gave myself away loving every minute, mind you. I became more weak, and it slowly broke me down till there was nothing left of me. So these days I am learning how to meditate my next move. I fell ill being that my body, mind and soul was in disease. I have dedicated my life now to what is right for me and my loved ones will be better off for it. I practice and work as a holistic life coach.

"As a holistic life coach and someone whom has been touched by endometriosis, I am on a journey once again accepting whatever it is, to change me for the better. It is not easy to be vulnerable but *necessary to grow and understand myself and others better.* There is no right or wrong way to this. It is about the realism and authentic energy." My mojo is coming back as I dare myself to show up for my live journal daily. It is a commitment and I am facing a fear and uncomfortable truth. We are human not meant to be perfect yet we are holding within us a most interesting, magical divine purpose and our true identity. I am at the moment exploring new ground as an individual and a CHLC."

- Value you over money.
- Understand the idea of money.
- Choose your time wisely.
- Cherish your moral self.
- Meditate on your next move.
- Be present.
- Be caring to our land.
- Be thoughtful.
- Donate yourself for no return in favor.

What do these words upon action mean to you?

It is not till I looked at life in the words that I began to understand differently. I listened to what they were trying to tell me. Remember that saying *"Sticks and stones may break my bones but names will never hurt me"*?

I understand why something in these words resonated with me and just maybe the sane has a secret meaning in it, like a clue and my new impression

Treat others as you want to be treated.

—Unknown

I have discovered it is always personal when working with people.

Sticks and stones will heal after a while and the words I find, will save me.

To take things people say or do personal, I believe is our true intake we believe of ourselves and hearing unpleasant things strikes a nerve. This should be taken in by those whom find themselves hurt. Nothing is ever said that we do not need to hear. We must not condemn another person for the ill they speak.

For to be defensive is to be struck by a truth we need to face for it will mend us to face the ugly. It sometimes takes another to stir up a negative, we hold inside. Walk away and reflect.

If it so passes that truth does not find you well perhaps you need to recondition your beliefs.

Heal, transform your derogatory shadow, and come into the light where it will soothe your state of being and mend in your healing.

For in meditation there is no gravity as we know it, just you and the light. Light as a feather I float, trusting in my Divine to hold me up.

Through a breathing practice and inner being.

A natural healing, coming home through meditation.

"a meditative silence"

Replenishing, recharging, regaining strength, clarity, healing. Sleep, rest, take in nature. Stepping away from the everyday noise. Adjusting your emotional channel, creating a tranquil frequency. Tuning in to what is more important at the moment for your well-being, and all those who need you.

I have done this at times, all of my life and never knew until recently what it was. I believe it is part of a natural state of healing, being.

Similar but not so eloquent as a monk taking a vow of silence. I highly recommend this act of meditation.

For truth is,
when I found my body
abused, used, and broken
by people, natural disaster or childbirth
Always there
to guide me, protect me, warn me, believe in me, ask of me,
words are there
in those very words *emotion* behind them breeding new life,
in good and bad words
it is up to the receiver to pay attention
take responsibility
this is where compassion and security in knowing what is right
through the heart they meet.
Signs embrace the light
for if we ignore the truth
the words will be construed, twisted
victims of negative entity
involve its nasty self in haste
we will lose the truth.
If one cannot speak
there is still "a feeling" in true

words turn to symbols become energy
electrified into divine magnetic occurrence
when it comes down to words spoken
listen with your whole heart
look into the very soul speaking, *to you.*
Be still for a moment, before you react
try to feel for yourself what truth be theirs.

Daily Practice in Human Conscience ˈkän(t)SHəns: an inner feeling or voice, sense of one's inner voice—*truth from the heart.*

Always must we ask our self questions, it helps keep us humble and true. Anyone can get off track, it is normal to stray from decency. Like working out, eating healthy, giving ourselves rest or tending to your garden.

Connecting with spirit, praying and meditation. Practice in the mirror, with a friend. Love a pet or take a walk, whatever works for you in staying true, *do it.* It will save you from a messy life.
Clean your spirit like, as you would sweep the floor!

When is the last time you gave someone, anyone your undivided attention?

How often do you complain about litter bugs or carts at a supermarket in a parking spot as your pulling in. Do you stop to pick up the trash or take the cart back to the rightful place, just because?

A reaction makes for the same action in turn.

What distracts you from connection with another being, be honest with yourself, it matters.

The very love of my dogs, looking into their eyes and feeling incredibly in love and satisfied. Animals and their unconditional saving love. All animals, they have this incredible magic about them.

Have we been so distracted. I can't help but sense heaven all around me these days the more in tune I become in my being the more I feel closer to an enlightened freeness. DOG turn the words around and you get GOD is that not a coincidence maybe for some but not for me. That is how my brain works. *What would even make me think that?*

We make bills, pay bills, go to work day after day, fall into routines, record TV! But yet we find it hard to believe in mystical moments or see butterflies following us with glorious tomorrows. Thinking our dream last night of a loved one, meant nothing, the beautiful and meaningful conversation we had with someone earlier in the week, *that we doubt?!* Stop by and feel for the truth until you stumble upon a lie. Be a detective and search for meaning instead of turning someone in for hopping a fence, for a short cut to school.

Adults become unglued and allow society to instill fears about their neighbors, for fear every time will hurt you and if *you dare be brave you just might be saved!*

Love instills love and hate breeds more hate. Something to think about . . . I have proven this theory true through my own life, actions, and observed it up close and personal! Again, it is simple mathematics if you ask me math being not my strong suit. Adding up truth every time comes out even. Good will is; what we all our attempting to achieve in our own lives, is it not?

A Negative response to life will have consequences unfold. All in all, it is not a matter of life and death for it is all a journey. It will just prolong your happiness, in your life and in the eventually in the lives of others. Deja vu is there to remind you. Your heart always knows better, it does. It was made with the intention to guide you right. The fuse sometimes needs maintenance. Our body is mechanical, be the mechanic. You are equipped with knowledge seek the tools so you may attend to the right parts that will work internally for the new improved you.

It is in the man who cares for himself to reap glory in happiness free of pain.

Changing oneself is not meant to erase nor delete a version of; only is change meant to grow and evolve one in spirited sense.

CHAPTER 4

Love Truth

The more you *listen*, the better you hear.

The time is now to pay attention.

If you are still and silent—a quality most of us come to find uncomfortable, awkward or a feeling of being in an unnatural state, I assure you this feeling you are having is normal and it is learned and happily can be unlearned with practice, patience and will. We are accustomed to know noise and are sewed into distraction. Once you can bring yourself out of the everyday and bring yourself inward and silence the commotion only then will you know the possibilities and come to see the beauty in you and all around you.

Where we come from or who we once were. Who people think we are, even in who you have come to believe you are. I can tell you this; if you believe that there is more and accept where you come from and assume responsibility for your actions there is a freedom and a life worth living and it is waiting for you. You have within you—skills, abilities, beauty, imagination, intelligence. Take the dare and get a life makeover.

You have a choice.

"To truly listen to someone it tis most important, a gift to yourself and another."

Truth is we are energy believe it or not underneath all this physical matter we are the most beautiful and exquisite source of energy.

How you perceive yourself is the question?

When you allow negative emotions to attach to your energy, it forms a kind of disease. Break down disease and all it means is your body, mind, or soul is in a state of DIS-EASE, get it? I have heard this before but when I stopped and applied this theory to my own state of healing I found it was accurate. By filtering what I hear and listening to what it is my body is telling me, is where I find truth and healing.

Your conscience will bother you terribly if you go against what is natural. Trouble is how do we decipher the difference, we are programmed to feel obligated by others, their hopes or demands for us of us. Our loved ones often want what is best for them yet they think it is for us. When we follow our dreams or our heart, we are given guilt trips and persuaded elsewhere.

Strangers with bad intentions and selfish desires also prey on those whom have a conscience. We all have one not all of us our in touch intuitively. That is why I urge you to study your mind, body, and soul for yourself, get aligned with your true identity and *think for yourself.*

Break down the gross matter that has caused you to stray from your true essence. Underneath the layers, think of it as a seven-layer chocolate cake. Many layers of negative that have massed over *love.*

Break down the gross, beginning with hate, sadness, disappointment, shame, loss, abandonment, anger. You will be happy to know you are still capable of being love. It is like changing the channel, you don't like the show you're watching then click!

True Identity

"We are not what we have done but simply who we choose to become, that matters."

Excuses insane merry-go-round, round and round *when will you stop and hear yourself telling more lies.*

Think of yourself as a magnet being pulled by or gravitating toward.

What do you choose, to be pulled or gravitate toward?

Unconditional love
believes in all possibility
In who we are meant to be.
First must we be still
Nor we judge the life of our brother
For the weak, forgotten, lost and strange
All who need patience, love, and understanding
For to judge a man means to one day walk in his shoes.
So my friend choose don't be the first to lose
"This every man is you."

It is okay to miss the love you call home
But not to travel is to die alone
Without you in my life is misery and dread
I feel no longer, I am
On this road is something I must do
yet I feel not quite together
For I fear one of my feathers
you dearest, love.
The one whom lifts my spirit ever so much higher

When we are near it is like electrical waves
through me, stimulating my very being.
You listen, you love in a way
I need to be felt.
I, strong and you are eager.
Venting for I will not *die*
Darling, know you and I are forever
Till our paths cross once again
we have the moonlight in a dream.

There are days I cry my heart out
the sadness coming from somewhere
buried deep within my aching soul.
You see as we heal
we remain aware of our emotions, continue to feel
it leaves one open to wounds.
I do not have all the answers for if I did I
would give them up to you now.
My eyes swollen from my tears.
Sadness lasts for days
how I long for timeless afternoons
dancing on the moon, singing love songs and kissing till dawn
how I long for you.

When we come to love ourselves in truth we then have the
ability to love
others unconditionally.

Be open to love . . .

"True Love always and forever
only because it grows and changes with its one soul."

We are accustomed to think we must be with the person for some time
spent and after the fact moved on from. Physically we do move on but the
heart never forgets. Expression of the two is sewn in and the thread like

the beautiful reading you will find on the next page. There are many loves. Sometimes we need several to learn, grow, change and feel the truth of love in which we almost always do.

"Friendship does not tell time, cost a dime merely it tis a reflection of love's divine."

— *Soulmate*

We are looking in the wrong direction for a complete love. Perhaps it is not in one person but in many. We must know to be complete . . . is to die. To love completely is to live without judgment, rules, or false impressions. To give love is to know love. To have a soul mate is to know the very Soul reading this. Do you know yours? Will we ever understand what it tis to love a Soul unconditionally without judgment, control or desire but to love and endure the very essence of its raw and pure nature?

"True love is not about two people but made up of all the love you find in your heart to forgive, understand beyond human reality, to love beyond measure and reason."

Love in the rawest nature of pure intention, for it tis never lost but safe in the heart of one.

"Romance love just might lead us to true love and put us on a journey in embracing our true identity, our purpose. Love may bring us more than one partner to grow, teach and bloom each other, is it worth the loss that will come? Yes, in the great loss there will be a rebirth of eternal grace. We know this to be, we yearn continuously. Deny it, it tis true love—sacred and alive within you and within me, forever."

How do you come to understand the meaning of true love?

"Everything comes full circle, someone special once shared with me."

"An invisible thread connects those who are destined to meet, regardless of time, place, and circumstance. The thread might stretch or tangle. But it will never break.

— This quote is thought to be from an Ancient Chinese Proverb. Author is unknown

I am grateful to them for sharing it, as I, now share it with you.

I didn't quite understand at the time what it meant. I came to understand in time, as all things do.

When we are ready, the journey and all the beautiful words that become angelic messages. Sharing with us connecting us to each other in ways we deny because the truth is told to hide. *"Thank God"* for those who listen, speak and share.

You are meant for someone it just might not be the way you were programmed or planned on.

When it is time for souls to meet there is nothing and no one that can prevent this cosmic interlude no matter where in the world they may be destined for all that their love is worth.

Time Coming Full Circle

Later on, in years to come this message came to me and instantly it clicked.

Beauty is in the obvious yet we turn the other way. The message being the circle of life on the merry-go-round, the idea *in everything comes full circle* is true balance in harmony and riding the vicious circle, how and when to get off notes. Finding one's key is relevant to one's own happiness.

O The circle of life. A shape in an energy field. It is open and can be also known as a thin line connecting each living thing to its source. A core if you will, and it resonates everything good. The outside is where you must be careful crossing, I like to think of it as a link in time traveled, now let me be clear I am not claiming this as a fact, this is my own personal theory in belief. Past, present, future unto now, the infinite destiny as my present moment. "As I am writing these very words in the present you are reading them in the future in which is your present moment in time."

It is in my lived experience that I have found clarity in visiting my past. It is clear I am found in my present. I have traveled through brief future notes and that is how I come to a divine knowing of what is true, real and sincere.

At the time, a dear friend came to need these very words, to hear them gave her peace. Because of something wonderful in the universe, I was able to pass it on . . .

We do not own anything it is for us to share, to connect another to its infinite place with the divine

source. For no one is lost that chooses to be, if you want to be found just ask.

Be patient, for *God is always on time.*

I say "God" because for me that is who my Source is, he is love. I was raised Catholic by religion but I am on a spiritual journey learning about what it is to be one with God and Nature. It may be different for you. Religion is a lifestyle, I have shared in with some of them and do not judge or do believe myself to be someone's jury on which one is right or wrong yet I am intrigued with their beliefs and truths. We must be open to all things that come our way for if it is in front of us we are meant to learn of it, something new or perhaps come to know Peace intimately.

War has separated men for the very beliefs, in cruelty of judgment.

"For to be Holy is to rain from all Divine Love and to shower all living things

with compassion, thought conscious love and free spirited generosity of heart."

Leaving one relationship for another. For all the times, I thought I was giving up on a job or relationship, truth is I did not give up I proceeded ahead through my Faith. There was more intended for me and those I was called upon to help. Giving up by definition would have been staying in place and giving up on my calling to purpose. I chose the hard road indeed, in retro I breathe easier these days and my heart is better content.

Nobody gets left behind only do we choose to encounter our better selves and walk in the way of light.

Relationships: think of it as a ship, a ship has a team (mates). Take care of each other and when the time comes when your service is over. Find it in you to wish them well as would a good captain, remain humble, and remember to truly love is to let go and have faith.

Purpose of a Partner

Sometimes God brings two people together. It is not about the question why but the purpose he has in store for us. We can deny all we want what the most important things are. Yet what it is—the most important reason for all of it . . .

All we can do is reach and believe it is for the greater good, in which we all want

happiness, love, and peace.

Do you agree?

"We venture out of our relationships when we start to grow restless with ourselves; it has nothing to do with our partner."

Just a thought? What is your view?

Change your *frequency* and be a *love vibe*.

Vibrate love, practice it, act on it, and express it every chance you get. This frequency will inspire others. Change your channel to positive love vibrations, you will find a most gifted treasure within your deepest, most authentic self. It is safe awaiting you to begin again or maybe for some of you who think you never had love, trust me you did and still do!

"When you love purely, your soul is open to love."

In relationships, each one supplies the truth needed to go on. To grow in oneself, a partner must fit in with the motive love has for each of them. I was thankful for my second marriage for it gave me time, understanding and unconditional love. A chance to know me, personally without trying to control me or love me too much.

Visiting a place of love within another being is like traveling through a time and space. Be present enough to genuinely receive the gift you have been given from one heart to another all there is and all there will ever be.

Loneliness is to be trapped in an emotional state while being alone is a chance encounter with our inner most sacred self, reap in all its wisdom.

To love you simply because you are a miracle. To find love within is a journey we make through one another.

I hold each love
for one without the other I would not be
in my heart intention grows
God holds each one of us
For his creation is made of love
For every time I walked away
Growing out of each life, that is how it felt, every time.
I never know when God will move me once again
It was not a question of love being present

more of a knowing and trusting
I am part of something bigger than
and when I look back
I see families that would not be there if I had remained in place
God knows better and I trust in
Because for every life I have lived, I have gained more than I lost.
It warms me when I think how true love has bloomed
and provided others with prayers answered
So how could I weep for love lost
in place seeds multiply in more love shared
For one day I will know of magic tis my fairy tale
till then I await my place in heaven, a place I call home.

We all seem to be looking for that one perfect person, but what I found, there is no one person. This blew me up because as I am a romantic and I do believe in true love of a lifetime and the fairy tale that does exist! I do buy into that still after *an engagement,* two marriages, and a love affair of the heart. Merely my perception has changed, and I see more clearly now. The big picture if you will. Since I can remember I have adored love. My parents were always showing their love for each other, they were not shy about showing affection and how they loved each other passed on to my brother and I.

My family, intermediate and extended were very close, my grandparents were undeniably wonderful and my Grama Yolanda whom I believe was perfect in her own right. I was showered with love and imagination.

Let me get back to the point here, I was born unto love, believing in the love of family. I was surrounded by an energy and it encouraged me to grow. On the flip side, later on in life, I experienced for the first time, *hard times!* Life lessons showed up and broke my home it also cracked something, in me. I was engaged and to be married, the most exciting time turned into a mission to save my family. There was no way we were going to be lost I believed in them even if they did not anymore. Unfortunately, this was a huge strain on my relationship. So the moral of the story is I sacrificed my happiness for the love of my family I did what I needed, knowing inside it was the most important thing. I had a choice at hand and needed to fulfill my purpose. I believe in love so why would it lead me astray?

I am here many years later to share the light with you. This is not meant to be a biography so this is in short. Love has never failed me. It is not people I have come to trust but love and God is love.

"Always following my heart and trusting my gut." There being a reason why I had to experience hard knocks, falls, ills and loss of love. Writing this book sharing my personal thoughts, theories, and feelings with you. My love for those whom shared their hearts with me, still very much alive and well. I feel good knowing that others have been blessed because of the trust I put into love and God.

It may not be perfect science or even the fairy tale. "I still dream in my heart" Love is to be shared and some of us need to go about our missions and do the work while others stay in place, a home base. I am not an expert just one whom has seen the positive impact every time life changed for me and I had to leave one place for another. My heart is full and heavy at times, I fall week and I am sad for days at a time except I have no regrets and know without one shadow of a doubt people are worth the sacrifice and I will continue to live every moment reaching higher for the better. Love has not changed me for the worse even with all the hurt and loss.

Evolve in love.

Love came when I needed it most, a heartfelt prayer to my grandmother upstairs. Looking up through a tiny window feeling scared and helpless crying bloody tears for hope to arrive. It only took days before he was there. A stranger with a natural comfort and ease giving me his hand and understanding. Without condition and without manipulation. Hope was there in place of man.

"Looking back it was the love that saved me, rescuing me from myself."

What about my plan? The timing was all wrong. My heart and my head were at war. Confused more than ever. I felt the connection not sure what it was for I never had feelings without the control of my own content this was not me or *was it?* Different than before. It was so natural and real like a dream inside my head, and my heart seemed to know him. He surely did know me, understood me, and wanted me, just for me and no other reason. An unexplainable love, so easy. He came to me like if he was sent . . . *special delivery.*

All I had to hear from a source I knew dear, eluded by these words "One man is your fate and the other your destroyer." This would change everything, for fate would accompany us on a road less traveled.

"Love can only make us better
Hate is what changes us for the worse, therefore
I choose love."

Fear cannot exist where love resides, fact.
Throw your fears away and be carefree, in love.

"My best of friend, whom I miss to this day. For the love we share is true and kind. The day I left everything behind. He found his family and now new life emerges to breathe new days. For he will continue on. I send him love for I am humbled by the kind of love he shares with another."

CHAPTER 5

Humility

I*nstead of passing on a rumor, pass me around—said Love*

May you know Humility
By definition:
the quality or condition of being humble; modest opinion or estimate of one's own importance

"Born to be different in a world subjected in learned and observed behaviors."

Conformed thoughts, wrong ways that pattern a man.

Be wary of self-absorbed and programmed intentions—*falsified, opinionated, controlled, wrong intent by love sources.*

Religion, tradition, politics on equal control—insecurity, broken spirits, love lost, abuse on nature. One has been manipulated by pain, sorrow, insecurity, anger.

Trust in true humility: "One may rust its weary Soul for to trust in oneself it takes a special role. Lie to yourself spins the truth out of control for now that told lie is true to another.

For now is the time to look into the mirror for truth needs practice and a strong kind of dare. Color the coating anyway you like but trust comes as wide as you wake."

Be humble in who you are, no opinion asked of you. Know your importance, he is counting on you. Your highest self is flawless, immeasurable amounts of love, you have within your heart. Be humble my friend in who you really are.

Expression, the very thing you talk of positive words of glory it is sanctuary.

Do not be a contradiction, meaning when we are out of balance with the very words we preach.

Truth

Waiting to exhale.
The same reoccurring thought has me over and over, thinking.
I am sure this *is* something of importance.
For why it is there nudging me to pay attention.
I patiently wait, keep going about my day accomplishing what it tis I set out to do.
Being in the moment free for the very thing that is meant for me.
Humbly awaiting . . .
Feelings embody me for *love is coming my way.*
Breathing in catching my breath.

Poetry
Dishonesty
December 13, 2007

When we start out we our full of light and peace, trusting we are, corrupted we become. By our parents, our friends, our loved ones at most. Some of us survive the madness, have a love, a "will" to be better. We our each other's symbol, idol, to reflect what is good what is right. We need to look at the stranger we pass on the street and remember with one word we are connected, again. With this truth there comes a responsibility to be honest to ourselves and our loved ones. What I see most of the time are thieves trying to deceive "one's" vulnerable heart. This is sad to me . . . What is not yours, treasure through the eyes of one you have not met here just yet, for if you steal what has not been given to you, remember what is meant will be of dust and will leave you with loneliness and for that I pray we reach down in and "will" our truth that has been there all along. Look with your heart not with your eyes. Trigger with the truth and you will be set free, from the madness that is now just a calm light breeze. Here

The Truth Will Set You Free

"So Jesus said to the Jews who had believed him, 'If you abide in my word, you are truly my disciples, and you will know the truth, and the truth will set you free.'"
— John 8:31-32, English Standard Version (ESV)

Denial

Looking for truth yet you still pursue denial
Lies untold truth unfolds
Standing still before my feet
. . . *waiting for you to notice*
Relish in what is
Dare beyond your limit set forth
For fear no longer holding your tongue
Pain grip your soul
No longer give it power
Release truth set yourself free
A mirrored image reflective upon the sun
"Glory Be"
Blame not man for a lie told unto you

POETIC LOVE FRENZY

Truth in a new dawn
Love be unfold.

"With All My Heart I Thee—
If you speak different than me, if you have fur
for hair, paws for feet. I just don't care.
If your skin is black, white or sunburnt red. I just don't care.
If you are born Muslim, Spanish or went to
Ohio State, please tell me more
For I love culture and learning different things. I just care.
If you dare to know?
I love you so and want to know more about you.
So judge me not I too
A Heart, a Mind, and a Soul
connecting, growing, living and loving.
I bleed too, red if you must know."

We are not divided by culture nor race yet what divides us *is* attitude.

Optimism is a sport for me, *a challenge to always find the right in a wrong.* A mission to go where others would not dare. This has taken me away from family, friends, and love. Great Sacrifices I have had to make for the greater purpose of those who need help. Once I dedicate my life to God, feelings of peace, happiness and a true connection enveloped me. There is infinity in those whom are in need, as I also learn, grow and become a better version. Each and every person put into my life, growing compassion on a deeper more sincere level. Finding and discovering the meaning *in love* and reasoning for myself and others. From this journey I accept with my whole heart. "The everything in nothing."

Facing fear straight on with love.

CHAPTER 6

Positive Insights in Being Loved

T he agenda in starting my day *is* kindness.

We all need kind reminders. I have a little chalkboard hanging on my door and I think of small things to write on it, just this morning I wrote, be kind. This may be silly to some but truth is we make notes for everything we have come to count on our mobile devices with reminders, dates and schedules, why not positive insights especially when we wake up heated or the pressure is building from every day details. It makes things right, and I would rather have a list of positive insights than a chore list!

It is a beauty of a day out, in this day be thoughtful and considerate in your travels. There is no need for speed for the road paves way for our loved ones. Be present in the moment. None of us want to hurt someone for being in a hurry or neglecting thoughts that may lead to tragic loss. Our dogs, mother nature's animals, children, loved ones they too walk this land. So put your phone down, it can wait, relax your foot from the speed that can harm another. Love one another, as you want to be loved.

POETIC LOVE FRENZY

"Love and gratitude will make for peace."

To humble oneself to another is to honor the presence of love.

Some days are not within her sight.
Alone walking in a world
that no longer looks or seems familiar, at times too familiar.
She hears voices, understands deeper than what meanings hold to others.
Energy has taken a new form of light.
No longer can she sleep.
Awake, for it is clear something bigger is going on . . .
A world that once was placed only now seems
to be a circle, round and round.
Purpose is the direction, light is the destination.
Love in all the stages
has made its way to surface,
there is no looking back because life is all a circle.
A choice has presented another time of wonder.
Darkness has no hold, it may linger yet will not likely survive.
Life continues to move its way, I can feel it nudge me.
Growing like a wild flower spreading light, the message is,
I can no longer sleep nor run lies
I will awake and be still for change once again.
Living strong within his light, I am.

Poetry is meant to be felt not exactly understood.

When change comes about and new ways are ahead, evil has a way of whispering negative nothings in your ear so stay clear my friends follow your heart and trust your gut for good is always here.

Promote what you love rather than bashing what you hate. Energy is magnetic, if you are shouting out your anger at something or someone in hate you are then no better than and in fact promoting rather than inspiring, understanding or simply creating a better way. Promote what you love and see what happens then perhaps, *love.*

We live in a world where we have falsely recognized the lie for the truth. A world where there are fake, unrealistic visuals all around. We want, we ask for but we contradict the very thing, truth!

Keep up with the Joneses, take a selfie, and don't forget the ultimate Photoshop illusion of yourself, for when someone meets you in person they may not recognize the version. You're rich in plastic but is your heart content for can you sleep at ease at night when you lay your head down, are you proud of the person who started and ended their day true. Will you dream pleasant or at all will you wake excited to start your day, looking forward to surprises and is love your way . . .

It is in the actual act in doing not in the failure
For to fail means you attempted to succeed.

"Be Love"
You want love
simply be love
You want peace
simply be peace
You want truth
simply be truth
"It begins with you."

One person connecting to another.

Finding a new way unto tomorrow
Never knowing what is to be
Looking back finding comfort in what was—
Yet they say there is no past to reflect
So what is this pulling me
Empty and alone
still I feel alive and well
Knowing something has me,
the light guiding this soul I keep
Does anyone know where tomorrow will go—

where will it lead
Having faith.
Until then
rebelling in emptiness
hoping one day I again
will be.

You want a truth here is one: it is not easy to see the good in someone especially when that someone is cruel to another or has had a bad rap. This is my truth, since I could remember I've always seen the good in people, born that way and blessed to have come from a non-judgmental background I must admit this did reflect positive influence on me as a human being. I was, in society standards, naive in my presence and spoken words yet pure of intention. I saw the raw and authentic beauty and love in people. Being that I am curious and wanting to know each and every person. My friends extended from all branches of life, personality and culture. My sixteenth birthday surprise party was the bringing together of friends and family and they had one thing in common, *me*!

Every era upon every age, from Rock n roll through to classical they were all there. I just didn't care. I love people and they love me back. It takes a strong individual and an open heart to see the good in people. It was not till I hit a rough time in life that I started to see the bad, the negative, the jealous demons people carried with them. I did experience anger, grief and jealousy at full throttle! I had my full share of demons and visited the dark side for a time. When I began on my search for truth I found wonder again, and it was more exquisite then I had ever known before.

Time would heal and love would be my mission once again seeing the pure gold in another being, even when they don't see what I see. I now living my purpose and introducing people to love, truth, and undeniable acceptance of themselves and others. So I believe I am here for a beautiful reason and the sacrifice that comes with, is worth it because God has my best intentions at heart. I am in good hands and so are you. So be true and see truth in the ugly.

Beauty resides in hidden treasures, just pay attention and it will reveal itself to you.

"Be brave in a new way of being true."

If it wasn't for your cruel intention
I would still be naive and blue
for it was you who brought to be, my truth.
I thank you, I do not hate you
For it t'was a time not a sentence
Within you now, a seed grows unconditionally, in love
Trust your instincts and love so much
and let thy will free your heart
Sow kindness, compassion and courage
Faith, may it help you share with every person
you have the privilege in meeting.

CHAPTER 7

Bridging Peace unto Your Past, Present, and Now

Making peace with your past is essential in the moving on healing stages. You must complete each part accordingly and face yourself. Looking at the ugly is a must in order to be free. You might have to change your belief system you have instilled for survival purposes, break your plans and ideas you set up and that notion you might know everything. It is not always because of others or up to them to fix what you, yourself need too. We are the masters of our own demise and the architects of our own happiness into the future.

Change your routine, make different plans how about no plans at all, free ball it! Be surprised by life.

We are accustomed to rules, they are set for those who still need them. Be different, set the bar for greatness to your best ability, be you. Rules were made to be broken, plans change for better things to come. This is not the first time you have heard this, but let it be the first time you listen and just maybe attempt to step outside of your bubble. The trouble you encounter is a reference.

God has lifted me higher so I may bring this to you, I am one who does not give advice, I have not myself taken. Filter the information, take it to heart, pray on it tonight. Just do one thing trust the light it wants you to radiate your truth. I know it is scary, it may even in fact sound crazy! What do you have to lose but yourself.

We are characters in a movie, create your fun, animate your love, radiate in your being, IMAGINE because you can! Everything in goodness survives the pain we intake whole. Be not lazy and weak minded. If you are brave, courageous and strong love will carry you through.

"Be love."

It is not about what you have *done* or *not done* but in fact, *who you are.*

For judge them not for their flaws
but acknowledge their wonderful
the very thing that drew you to them
Be not jealous for you are a reflection of each other
A perfect blend ingredients
for what he does not have,
you do and for she the beauty, you are the wings
Fly high and know your worth
for we are all one, in the same worth
think in color, be of light
rid the shadow of deceit
forever a friend.

Finding a new truth with every love story
More of a journey with self
Finding different perspectives, motives, and insight
within my soul discovering real beauty for all
Each and every moment I more free
Love is true yet meant to be in a way
Completely enlightened by how it feels to be me
Loved with such honesty
My heart beat getting more intense with each reflection Looking back at an old version of me, myself and I

What does it all mean . . .
The story is not yet over only just begun
A love for me, for you, for ye.
"Looking back on love"

It was when I looked back unto my past life that I saw lives being connected only because I dared walk away. Children loved, provided for, given a chance, a family. For this did not mean they were spared from pain. It meant they also had divine plans of purpose, meant for them. Because I was blessed with such love of family, I would never want to deny a child that truth, and special beginning.

A child born upon new life would extend from a man who loved so strong. God knew he was meant to continue on, who was I to stand in front of such a grand plan? I, too, had a mission, a duty, for I am here now writing this book in words of true, sharing my story with you.

Love is real, family is true, and there is still pain in every blessing. You cannot hide from the journey that knows better. Prayer saved me more than once for every time I left a life, I was very much aware of everything around me even the love that still was present. Something bigger was moving me forward, I could no longer hold on, having to let go. I could not fight it and chose not to. I had my faith in love and praying lives would mend in time. There being great sacrifice in love's divine purpose for if you do it for the right reasons you shall reap all of the rewards in heaven.

I now know the meaning it holds and hold deep gratitude for my faith in trusting GOD.

"We will meet and the timing will be just right as it usually is when we are present."

"Persuasion has timing quarters and if you dare love from the heart in wholeness you shall derive freeness in truth."

Sometimes when you hear a message over again in repetitive nature only does it prove it has something more to share, with you. Like watching a movie, guaranteed you watch that same movie three times over *you will* notice something different you did not notice before and furthermore a message, a moral or value that at the time you watched it, you were in a different state of mind and now you see the deeper meaning.

> *Once love is,*
> *it can never be broken, lost, or forgotten,*
> *like the ocean meets the shore,*
> *like the wind calms a breeze after the storm,*
> *settling in a state of truth.*
> *Love can never can be undone,*
> *dreams we promise each other, forever*
> *because love is.*

CHAPTER 8

Greed

Freedom is free and thank God for the heart to see that. ♥

Free yourself

"If you don't let change visit your life, kryptonite will invade your space with no invitation."

You do not need a status to prove your love nor worth!

Work for money and you will find yourself broke.
Remember to look unto your pure of heart's intent
and know your mind for it can will your Spirit.
Come to honor your Soul for this is why he holds you in his
palm for all thy be good and all thy will never be without.

Love is not to be owned for if you take ownership you do not have love's best interest at heart yet to save the feelings of goodness it will give you freedom of spirit then will it offer abundance.

"It is not a privilege to have love, or beautiful things nor in having the good life within it is merely a gift from someone whom believes, in you and loves you, true."

To love someone for who they are and not for who you want them to be.

Imagine a world you took pardon in destroying, all who knew better. Would you still be pardoned? If life whispered in your ear, it is you "the one" we need you. Would you in fact stand up and set forward in action first stating love as a truce.

An Exercise

Closing your eyes at this very moment. Take a nice deep breath in. From your heart, say aloud thoughts that spoke true. It is irrelevant what truth you have formed let this moment free you. It is in fact, the feelings that hold dear. Feeling what your heart is telling you, once you have taken the time to listen is groundbreaking, fly as high as your wings will take you . . .

I

For what tis yours only dust and as one can see when placed in the palm it may only find it has slipped through with one touch.

Possess not materials nor gold in turn, if you so choose to, you may come to find you are the one under possession.

Take with you a memory anytime as you wish *for all your heart holds true; yours in the glory of thy own divine.*

II

What mine be yours, yet yours be mine.
The truth shall yearn
instill in you until each own dying.
Prosper in truth and it will in turn
inspire that in all its worth.
Touch with purity and kindness—
This it will come to save you.

Peace it is, you hope for
ask and it shall be.
Listen patiently thought sounds of light run through you,
Be still, be love, listen for it is trying to tell you.
Give with thy own
pay close attention
Radiate love vibrations
for it does not cost in consequence
receive a healing
Come, share, smile upon a new horizon, yours be true
For what is yours is only of dust.

May the ocean tide meet up to your expecta-
tion and for the first time may you see
in the truthness of beauty the view. It has to offer
The wind wipe anew truth for your soul is
clean on the forever shores of heaven
Allow today's magnificence to take your sorrow
and radiate pure light throughout your body, mind, and soul
Do not fear in what you will lose
be grateful in endless pleasure excited for what there is to gain
always my love.

For man need not in things but seek comfort in his truth.
For I now below the poverty mark and the cost will be mil-
lions spent.

Let yourself be not a hostage to another but a forever friend.

Love without condition
Give with no strings and secure your peace of mind for you've done
good.
There are no rules just one's morals, the value is in knowing
you can lay your head down at night and find contentment. Is that
not the ultimate reward?

I found it is, to lay my head down at night with no regrets or feelings of dread that I have hurt another with untold truth, lies, or half-truths.

This does not mean I am innocent it only means I have decided to live a life true to myself. And to cause ill to another for profit, personal gain or selfish desire is not what I am about. We do not know what surprises life will bring or the lessons that will be needed. The quiet notions we whisper or love in which we still hold deep down inside of us. I have come to the conclusion that what is, simply is, there are things we can control and others we have to live with, it is how we proceed forth that counts.

> *"Make friends to grow tomorrow*
> *make love to know peace*
> *for there is plenty*
> *Fear not in a lie told unto you*
> *So you may steal from others and sleep in a vegetable state*
> *For money is of paper and paper comes from trees, in that tree is your*
> *wealth of purity, richness in the hands of the man who believes he can*
> *crossing meadows wide as rivers*
> *You my friend are made of this very land*
> *Carry love in your heart and kindness the change in your pocket*
> *And when they tell you to give back respond with a smile*
> *For a smile comes from a place*
> *A language we all speak and understand*
> *Sing it with love and dance, as if you will never be without."*

Ego vs. Spirit

Ego: Man made.

Derived from darkness eluded by anger, sadness, loss, fear, jealousy, insecurity. Fear holding you back, lies instilled. Seek the truth for a better side of you.

Fermented tales drawing us away further and further from the truth that will save.

Holding one hostage because what feelings or wealth they comfort you with.

Spirit: a childlike innocence

Forget what they have told you.
Now is the time, make it count, have the will to rewrite your story.
Only to then understand your earlier life.
Find the freedom so you may finally live true to your calling.
Born unto dream only to be put asleep.
They whom have instilled lies masking truth for tales.
I urge you turn away from the ills that distract
be still for you are not more an adult than a precious child within.
There's one truth it is high as the clouds seem close and far
as an ocean seems deep, a sky filled with hope and wonder,
placed in your heart for safe keeping. Explore your potentials.
May your spirit soar here for it is your natural home.
With your feet safely touching the ground i give you my
blessing to simply close your eyes and with faith as your
guide allow yourself to free fall, life is awaiting you.
A divine purpose is your gift.
Give grand.

In search of courage

Ego said unto the girl, "*You betrayed me!*"
The heart of man with chills through his rough skin
A warmth somehow seeped through
from his lips and whispered
I love you for it is only sadness for your hurt
The mind thought quickly processing
What do they expect me to say, *how shall I act?*
Shall I express how they programmed me to act?
The Soul communicated understanding
Giving wisdom to the couple for their only question was why
us?

Transcend compassion and cultivate a new day, starting with yours truly.

Spirit knew why.

Love is the kind of fairy tale that blossoms here and then awaits our bloom in heaven.

I cannot take credit for this sane below but thankful for those whom have shared it. I have come to listen and understand what they mean, applying these truths in my daily life.

"Assume nothing for who does may be taken for an ass."
— Unknown

Be Brave

When we allow fear to set in, it will then have the ability to trip us. In that very fear we lose sight of what is true and what is right. Breathe in through your heart and close your eyes. Take a nice deep breath, one at a time, begin to feel relaxed. Remember you are a person of great potential and within you is LOVE. Fear cannot exist where love resides, fact.

It tis what you need to live, it is in you to be happy, create bountiful spirit in place of wealth.

Bankrupt your false beliefs on what it tis you need to survive, and be in peace.

Blessed be in the infinity of loving true.

> "In our own way, we can account
> for more than a dollar
> which will not pay for your life
> in love and friendship."

On my search for love, truth, and romance I found "I am."

For I am love

For I am truth
For I am

"In all thy of good of spirit rest assure my happiness. I carrying, in myself all along. I had to connect, the pieces, in those whom I have loved. In each other we live, we breathe, we grow in love and as it may; a deeper meaning of our stories we find, truth and what truth thus there to be known is being love."

My journey was just coming to an end and as I saw the road up ahead, a knowing that somehow it was for me. The light I was looking for was within me my whole life through and I was now aware how to find what it is I am looking for . . . . and what that truly means is; I am never alone, never have I been but in my own state of mind.

Each loving relationship and friendship has been connecting me to sacred self not derailing me but sending me off to the next port for I have more of life to visit.

Truth is, if you stand still it is not a penance but a compromise with no strings. These special individuals have the pleasure to stay in place and make for a home base to those who have to leave. These special individuals have a contentment, a loyal and spirited sense within to provide their loved one's security here on this Earth. I presume that is where this beautiful sane comes from. *"Home sweet home."*

"For there is no end just a change in scenery, energy and season. Those whom believe tomorrow is awaiting them thy divinity will wake new blossomed ways of truth. Beginnings so evident that always will there be a time to say *I love you* or *see you*, perhaps a feeling thy will be there to love, to share—with you."

CHAPTER 9

Love That Changes You

Love does not judge but simply admire, it adores.
Something to think about

"True love is not about two people but made up of all the love you find in your heart to forgive and understand. When you love so deeply tears, blood red falling down your cheek. Your soul crying out with all you've got, the thunders of heaven can hear you taking your last breath it may seem you can no longer breathe or move on. Pain that rips your flesh and yet there are no wounds simply the love that still yearns."

"True love is not about two people but made up of all the love you find in your heart to forgive and understand."

Sometimes love is telling the one how you truly feel and not tip toeing around! If you're pissed, tell him and hash it, so you can kiss it and make it all better! If she is annoying you, show her and be done with it, making up is so worth it! *"Do not be stubborn use your voice or lose your space."*

"Love is not merely an item to be possessed yet a spirited energy meant to be shared, lived and set free."

"The very thought of you warms my Soul
They said unto each other
let go, let go, let go
stay awhile do not leave so soon,
I need your love to bloom.
I fear
I am wilting for the thought of you not near.
A sign, I pray
For your seed feeds my Soul
The very thought of you
Know for now I love you still
where we are is planted in a garden
for true love warms the sun in bloom
let go, let go, let go
Till tomorrow will come soon."

What is happiness to you?

Happiness is:

Do you notice the i stands tall, that i stands for the very person looking for happiness. For me, I found happiness is; within me and people have added to my happiness. So if you notice now there is a Y in happiness, it is how i see it. Because once I found the true meaning of happiness: "HAPPYness stands out!" Get it?

Happiness is not a privilege it is a truth—we all have within us, find it at your will.

> *Happy is a state of mind! Entrusting those you care for, with*
> *your truth. Their compassion in sense will give courage, to be.*
> *Happiness is inviting love in thus keeping the door open,*
> *In being true to self, God will then protect you from harm.*

Love is love and who are we to deny someone of their next truth tale.

Be love and kindly move aside and trust in *God for to pray unto him he will tend to your heart.* Denying its life is to face unthinkable pain and confusion. Channel the truth so you may accept and honor thy love in its purest state.

CHAPTER 10

Forbidden Love

Friendship on fire would be the everlasting truth the undying never emerging relation between heaven and now. The one and only time a flame would be forever lit between two souls passing through–

"Falling in love is the happening when we are not trying so hard, it is there like magic."

Understand beyond human reality, to love beyond measure and reason. Loving in the rawest of nature in pure intent, a vow two souls promise for it tis never lost but safe in the heart of One.

When a dream brings you a surprise visit on a Sunday even if only for a moment.
(This is a true event)

When people have done special things for me, if it was a surprise bouquet of flowers at my door, or holding the door open for me, many small or big acts of kindness and love, they have never gone unnoticed always meant everything to me!!

As much as you may love and care for someone, when the time comes when you feel growth you must be aware of what comes with this feeling and approach it with heart and truth . . . You know the words need to come out . . . Fear has no place here. Where true love resides, growth is always present.

Experiences grow our spirit, even the bad ones. No blame to another; you may thank them later, for you will be better for the love you share will be true.

Marry for love, or settle for a platonic sort of love; true love cannot be replaced, yet love is love, and it always has our best interest at heart-

A Love Affair of the Heart

As time passes, the two shall meet. A Neverland reality, losing touch for just a moment. Their lives would take them elsewhere, a miracle instilled blessed in their dreams. Securing their love, thy would be given strength to go on. Woven threads of light sending them off. Friendship on fire, a flame burning in remembrance. For they were one in the same. When together it was obvious the connection between them. Miles would divide them only in the realm of denial, for they knew truth and that saves them from despair.

A question one day on Earth would come to divide them. Would he be her savior or her demise?

A Short Story

He was smitten and she afraid. She had never came across one with such intensity and sureness, in which *they were meant to be.* For her it was complicated she had a plan and the timing was wrong. He was patient, kind and strong. His love was real she could feel it throughout her skin and her heartbeat that pounded so loud she had trouble hearing over the sound of his voice. He knew her and oddly she knew him. But it would not be easy. She had become lost and her Faith was weak. Trusting him she took his hand. The road would not meet up to his liking and when he tried bringing her home, she did not meet his family's plan. She was forbidden and not welcome. He assured her it was not her and had a way of making her feel at ease. His strong positive sense would guide them. She loved him almost instantly but her conscious self did not let it be known. She never got over the thought of his family not liking her. She knew one day it would be made right and they would come to love her as their own. It would take time and lesson. "For a weed is nothing more than a flower hidden in bloom" They would continue on remaining in secret for their worlds were not the same but their hearts, their minds, and Soul were connected in divinity, one flame. Life denied the two access to living love together.

> *Given your love*
> *always on time*
> *merely does it change*
> *like a season*
> *a wind carries it North*
> *spreading it true*
> *seed for the land to grow*
> *endless amounts for all to enjoy.*
> *Love tis energy in light*
> *nurturing a truth of self*
> *to hunger no more.*

Sometimes words don't speak, a language, sometimes they have more to say, in expression.

I want to say I love you yet my feelings are quite indescribable. To look at you I feel fire and to say I merely love you well that would not do justice to the feelings that yearn in me truly, for you.

Maybe it is I never felt this way before so there are no words to explore . . .

We have heard the tale to say I love you is overplayed, used and abused. The explosion of desire only those entitled could decipher in its meaning be true.

"I love you" is said and done but to have a feeling one cannot put into words only to feel them for someone that love is one of a kind true, unspoken melodies solely yours and solely mine

yet when I hear you say the words from my heart I care you . . . my heart knows thy to be true may I say I care for you.

To take for granted and utter words just because or to save face from the truth loves tells. Words unspoken on behalf of love portrayed let our dreams share in the meaning for we do not need in words for feelings say it all.

C H A P T E R   1 1

My Thoughts on God

Ever wonder why we refer him as the "one"?

"If you want to know where to find the one, simply believe in you."

Purity of being in love the heart has everything to gain and nothing to lose.

"When you touch someone with your spirit and in return they touch your soul with their heart."
— Author Unknown, thought to be a spiritual quote.

What are the reasons you came to lose your faith in him? Is it time to look at it again. Find the truth for yourself. Search for love within you and find who is this God, Jesus, Ala source. For who is the one?

Places to ponder a thought, a religion, a church, a person, an organization, in the cemetery, perhaps in a dream. If your life is not what you want, I suggest you start asking, praying and looking for the answers .... For your heart's intention will set you up. You are worthy and never let that stop you from finding him, asking and praying for your life. If you find your life's a mess maybe it is time to face the ugly, the pain that grows distraction in you.

What blame placed caused you to stray?

Taking Responsibility
Making every moment count. Inspiring hope, love, and compassion to all whom seek out. Writing, speaking, and living the raw and beautiful truth. Living the life God wants for me and while I have been hurt I still have a beating heart that loves more now than I ever knew was possible. An open heart loves true. For the secrets of my Soul whisper healing notes and I am again free to live happily within my sacred self touching those with inspirational thoughts that soon turn to light.

"For no man is abandoned by God seek your truth and you will find you are home."

What God takes away he *in return* gives in splendor.
For man has took from you not God for he resides in you.
Love yourself and be free.
Ask for help.
Seek out guidance.
Change your channel and tune into faith.

To look outward will frustrate and postpone for it is within us to seek inward, and turn your positive light on and allow it to show you the way.

"We throw blame when the pain is too much. Being human, a nature to make others responsible for something gone wrong? Tossing all clarity away with lies mixing blends of disastrous illusions unto the wind, ricocheting self-delusion and then soon destruction. When we blast God for he has done this too us, when in fact it is us. We must look in the mirror and stop the madness we have to each take responsibility for living a better life by taking care and loving ourselves better! Life is a game, wake up and think differently, you want a better life reach out and change things up, stop with the pity party. Take your losses and use them to your benefit as they were meant to condition you not for you to role play the victim!! We are all broken and it is our mission, the very reason we dwell to heal each broken piece through patience and love."

"God said trust in no man yet do love every
man and this very man is you."
—Unknown

When I proceeded in letting go and stopped trusting in man I started to trust in God more and came to find out he is enough. When man disappointed me, I decided to grow more within myself.

I will speak on this subject;
I remember someone very close to me once said; men lie because when we tell the truth women never let it go and then tangle the truth worse than if men just simply told a lie. Boy did that make sense! SO, I worked on understanding truth, what it means and how it affects us.

I looked at him, and at that time, I was soul searching so it stayed with me. Since then I have been on a mission, a truth mission trying to understand why we lie, and how did we start? I used to pride myself on the truth and yet there were still colored tales. I remember growing up until now hearing and telling all types of lies black and white lies, fibs, the grey area, color coated lies, half truths. All lies, illusions, beliefs, tales, stories, sorts of reality. We are all guilty of such misbehavioral truths, for all different reasons but truth is, it is never a good idea to lie and it only perpetuates more hate and unhappiness.

I believe and I am thankful what his truth and wise words spoke, it makes sense. I have found so far that truth is available to those who want it for themselves and are not afraid to hear what needs to be said. It is in the brave and fearless, the ones we stand to hate or feel betrayed by when the truth comes out it usually causes conflict even pain. Friendships are lost and more lies are added to save whatever evidence of truth, they with stand to keep.

One example: I would like to illustrate into words is, when your girlfriend asks, "Hunny, do I look fat?" For one, no woman should ever, in my opinion, ask that question. It is toxic and loaded. I can view it from both sides. I myself have asked a question similar to that. It is not fair to either party. I am going in on this more than I would like. So here it is, if you don't want the full truth, don't ask for it. Ladies and gents always know your worth, it is in the question where truth is set free or made hostage.

If we lie to ourselves then the truth will always be false if we are honest with ourselves, truth will always reign and we shall be free in living, loving and being in the good life within. Period!

For in the words of God sometimes we need reminding. To hear something is the first coming and to listen is the believing and in the actual doing is and finally we sit, breathe in through our hearts and be thankful for we are loved that much to be reminded once again.

I speak from the heart, to those I have hurt from my lies told, it is in forgiveness that we come full circle in love and truth. Think of it not as already said and done but a kind reminder to hear it, process it and act upon. Listen to what it is trying to tell you, something of great importance. For if you hear it again, it is because you maybe need to listen.

He is within you to recognize your weakness and strength.
To defend from evil not from that in which has only
love for you, knowing you are deserving of. You have
not been neglected only spared from that of what wants
to keep you sad, angry and confused. Come to believe
in your truth for you are what you seek in love.

"A prayer is a poem of love, seeking help, good thoughts, healing, saving for whatever you are in need of, even if it is simply to say thank you. Beautiful words for they have power in the act of prayer. To emphasize such love and energy for another is; to be love everlasting, exquisite healing and miracle in prayer."

I have a prayer at this very moment, and here it is. My heart with all that I am through love, pray that we think before we speak, love more before we close our hearts and most of all take a deep breath in before uttering words of hate out from our lips. "May lips be for kissing, words spoken from the heart, as when we were children when all we knew was love, laughter and freedom- "Be Love" through diversity, because that is what we all need more of, act upon your wishes for they will free your Soul. I stand tall for all humanity, all of nature, all who walk this land, separate we are not.

For the day came when I knew GOD was enough for me. Through him, I am the best version of myself. When I, most desperate and afraid he lifts me up and protects me from harm.

CHAPTER 12

New Horizon of Conscious Thought

Society has ruled in favor of status since far back as we can remember. Our place in history reigns on religion, politics, family, tradition. Evolve from fear, be fearful not my friends for there is something better, something that will not harm our souls and drown us in misery. Here we are in the twentieth century and still we walk among what is right for others for all the wrong reasons, a madness that has spread like disease. It tis what ills us, it breeds. May your heart rule over all that remains to be true. The time has come when we stop controlling the thoughts and hearts of our loved ones and allow what nature has in store. Trust that, a natural flow and all will be right. Have Faith and allow love to be restored as it was meant.

Be the cure and share this healing.--------------------♥

The world's sadness makes for incomplete restlessness . . . for we are not of this place must we wake and believe we are enough to make all right within ourselves first.

Why do we hide from a love so true yet run straight to something that makes us blue.

In truth there is hurt but also there comes freedom.

"When love trips you and it feels like you're drowning in a sea of blue."

Age of the young at heart, to say *old people* is an outdated saying.
grow with new vocabulary, a new age, a new dawn.

> *We are all growing in one way or another*
> *In facing age be true to yourself*
> *"Timeless is the beauty that holds love before anything else"*
> *Swing from life, holding your breath, wish-*
> *ing upon a star and thanking the heavens*
> *thus you made it this far.*

Sending this out into the cosmos . . .

Thoughts of love even when not deserved of shows truth in oneself. In fact all you need is a good love vibe toward another Soul. I am finding on my journey that complimenting someone or giving credit and noticing one's work is incredibly important. Happiness arrives in our lives when we give. There is no condition on how much or less we receive back. Keeping score is for a game, such as football.

In the beginning no person warns us that we will be hurt, that we will lose loved ones.
All there is and nothing.
I say that is crap! We are on a journey and the beauty "is knowing" nothing is ever lost. Finding it in us to forgive ourselves, mostly. Can we really possibly hate? Once we look upon what it was that was taken from us only then can we begin to ask why and from there see with true sight of heart where we are and who needed us more . . . ?

This life created for us, bountiful and gentle with misery as our guide and transport.

Shield yourself from empty desire and "will" your being higher.
Believe in the child who yearns for your acknowledgement and love.
Allow thoughts of love to clarify what has been disarranged by illusion
from darkness.
Be the light for it will bring you peace.

Patience is what you will need, manifest every thought that is good
and toss the bad ideas into the void where they will be dealt with accord-
ingly. Save the best ideals, the warmest thoughts for you and give them away
as they are endless gifts.
Before you know it love will be present, a calmness will be evident.

For now, notice the trees for they are what provides the walls
to your home, the paper to your pen, a chair to lean upon first
love's kiss, shade from the sun and umbrella from the rain.
May the trees in all of Nature bring you great comfort.
Know they are wise and tall enough to whisper to the heavens.
For they keep your secrets and carry spe-
cial messages to a loved ones upstairs.
Be kind to Nature for tis your parent, your confidant.
A magical connection tuned in with the harmony of Earth.
For a flower will bloom and a car may cost you your fate.
Choose wisely and enjoy in the presence of forgiveness` if you accept.
Endless amounts of love you carry in a spe-
cial reserve, only you know where to find it . . .
Bless you on your journey and be kind for all whom breathe in
light, have a loved one in need of a love vibration in compassion.
Be clear in your thoughts and remember when the shit hits
the fan what will you take and who will you call?

Str8talk from the heart

To speak from the heart and voice my personal thoughts and what some would think of it more as the cold truth, to speak of and pronounce depth throughout the grey areas in one's life, is to free the air of toxicity. To be not afraid in hurting fellow man with the truth for freedom of the truth is the medicine that heals all wounds. No color coating: Intuitive response.

Stop making excuses, tell no lies for it is keeping you from reaching new highs.

Routine and consistency: not one in the same but both essential for moving along. In balance they play.

A little freedom too, don't be afraid to break some or maybe all the rules.

Everything we do responds to the energy we give it. Poker face in the eye of diversity.

Inner peace is the goal find within yourself and the world will resemble the very pace you set.

You must remain calm for if you are frantic your energy will become static and chaos will arise to the occasion. Be still and focus, transfer love vibes only then will you see clearly, what is true.

In balance we can come to enjoy our lives and be present for those whom we hold dear and furthermore all of the souls we come to meet on this journey.

Make it count this life of yours, derive a difference take the labels you wear and burn them with one flame that forever loves true.

Fate Remembers When

To trust **in** Fate is to never be disappointed, ever.
Trusting in my entire being gives me strength to move on.
Never far are we in Spirit from our Soul.
Loving and letting go made it so worthwhile
when I can truly help someone in my present moment.
If I stayed where I was comfortable
I would not have been there for that person in need.
Making a difference in someone's life;
to hear it in their voice, feel it upon your skin.
Is true happiness to me.

Passion, to be passionate for,

infused with pure intention
with great emotion
Never be owned nor controlled but shared in its entirety
In love.

Thoughts on Parenting from Someone Whom Has Been Around Children All Her Life

Be true in heart of a child. *Think again* before you let your hurt reflect on what is best for them. Stand tall and humble yourself when it comes to love with a child. Keep your personal feelings out of it. Maturity in conscious thought is recommended in showing love to a child. In a break up situation don't make them suffer for your messy life, or ideas. Compassion and understanding is something we all stand to recognize.

A few words to take in and think about . . . .

Are we using children as weapons against those who have hurt us, betrayed us? Is it fair to them, the children whom know only of love?

Children should not be used as targets or cameras, what do you think?

When they act out are they perhaps trying to get your attention?

"They are innocent so they perceive truth where we have lost ours, look to them . . . more than you do. Learn from them. They are love, so accept it and grow from these miracles born here to save the world."

We do not own them, find your happiness within their love and attend presence. Nay in making them pay for your sins or repeat in your failures. They should not be controlled or used. Love them, guide them, protect them but **know they are free to choose**, *they have been sent to do what is meant of them.* You have been blessed where some may not have had the gift to bear a child. Cherish their differences don't flee from them.

For families mend by sharing their loved ones with others for we are meant to love freely.

It takes a village to raise a child. (African Proverb)

I believe this to be true for myself and for children who later become adults themselves. Climb out of your box and be among truth. I am thankful for the mothers who came into my life for I, in turn shared their love to many and continue on their love, given to me freely.

For to have a child is the way; yet to raise one might not be meant, judge not, only be thankful for the gift.

May we be loved and break from creating war with ourselves, and others.

Be ever so kind to the earth for the land is your home
do not be fooled by the houses you build, the com-
forts of your decor the cars that you drive.
For to step on the land is to step on your son whom
is of the blood running through your veins.
Be true to your children for they one day will
reap the truth and love the way you do.
Be plentiful with your kindness and clean up after yourself.
Care for your greens as you would your car.
Provide the upmost respect for in the way you keep up in display.
If you must kill a bug first say a prayer for send it away with love.
A living breathing being is the reason we are all here.
Trust in Nature for it provides us with
color, scents, shelter and more.
The elements, the minerals, the gold that you wear.
It is of the land and you are it's borrower.
Be kind to yourself for if you care and I know that you do.
If it is not a brother, a sister, a mother or your one
true love, a child is in need of you to be there.
For you must find the truth to sew happi-
ness, it is within you and the land.
"Be love."

Stepping into Love

Or born unto love know it is still love.

"For I may not be a mother by blood yet I am mother to all."

For it does not take ownership nor control to guide a child yet true love and intention places high regard for well-being on to another.

Step parents, parents, remember the heart of a child *is* love and allow that be your guide.

Rose

"I loved her as if she was my own. The very first time she called me mommy, I felt my heart tender in that very moment. It felt so right but in a reality they would say it was wrong for this young child no older than four, so easy and so true this coming from her heart. How was this to be wrong? In telling her I would be her friend and love her as if I was her Mommy, always. Her eyes glazed over looking at each other as we shared a secret in truth."

Speaking on behalf of all sides I can seriously see the break in connection and how we are all subject to harm from being hateful and keeping a child from believing in love. Divorce and breakups are devastating for a child at any age and all those around family friends, even ourselves. A tear in our solar system, the idea of what love is needs to be restored. My prayer is that we remember what is important and put aside the ignorant and petty thoughts that break a family in true. May this parting grow us and teach us not divide us. Looks are deceiving, so be true in sincerity of a child this will reflect upon you.

These questions are meant to heal not persecute.

Have you given love without strings attached to your child?

Have you nothing left for yourself

Do you feel depleted? Resentful?

Jealous of your child? This is important to recognize.

Do you feel your child or children have stolen your youth, life?

Do you believe with all of your heart children are better off without love from their parents?

"To keep a child from their parent or grandparent is to control what will later cripple, a perception."

Are you a parent whom loves their child spite the money it takes to raise them?

A mother's love and their own inner happiness are to both be recognized for we are human still a girl now someone's mother too.

Brand your love not in what you do but in fact who you are, for you are many things

Do not box in your amount of talent, personality, and gifts you are holding within

For a mother is a friend

A brother, a husband

The husband, a teacher

The teacher, a woman's child

This child, a pet's best friend

Society will take away your power do not give in to the static

Stand alone in truth and others will dare to be themselves, too!

Judge Not for You Will Be Condemned

Can you honestly with good thought and reason deny a living breathing thing, being from this world or another—deny love, respect, understanding. Who are we to judge think, twice how little and ignorant one sounds when condemning another life.

Is it you who judges man or the man speaking ill. Contagious it is to listen to negative hate. Be a leader—turn an ear, be brave in your words and know yourself to be true. It may be scary at first every time you stand up to someone with good intention but I do it and it is an awesome adrenaline, scary every time but it feels damn good! And even if I do not get recognition, I see the good it did, to speak up. I will be faithful and serve God in all that is right and good, for evil has no place in my life.

I am not an expert nor am I, a doctor, I am not innocent nor perfect. I do not claim to have all the answers for they change all the time and for what it is worth, truth I do believe, in me and I have lived, for my experiences and people have been my teacher. God always by my side and the angels as witness to my truth. I am an explorer, an important part of nature I will protect her and her creatures. Who am I to harm them for without them we would not be.

The land feeds me, nature calms me and the waters soothes my soul. "Be love."

The man with too many excuses makes it only to the front door but will never be invited in.

Are your excuses keeping you from the very things you want most in your life?
Push yourself past the limits, when force is needed to break your meekness and replace it with boldness.

October 19, 1999
Midnight Poetry

Natural way of healing
Natural when things are right feelings are good
sincerity in every way
why is it we walk away
we choose the lie get carried away in a lie
complain we do forget not a beautiful natural way
here listen again
Natural in every way
remember this live this hold it within your heart
an intimate kind of kiss
give a hug with meaning allow for that healing

stay away from the thug who try to step and poi-
son our air for it is free and clear so natural
it needs not for chemicals and it is not for sale
Natural way of living.

Illness or Fate Changer

Surviving a chronic illness, health condition by tuning in to love.

An all-sustaining love in my life has helped me heal in more ways than physically. It has awaken a part in me, that sleeps. In its entirety I yearn for more. Growing impatient at times and insecurity invading my peace, wanting sanctuary from all the noise in my head. But only for a moment as I pull myself together to sound clarity for love always survives the bad, the negative, the ill. I trust in this every time. The condition for I do not own, only does it borrow my body for a time, to grow me where I am still weak and in need of wisdom.

A classroom in a dimensional time and space so I may grow and better adapt myself with the world and connect to my sacred self evolving within my power. Tuning into love brings me clarity. Balance, with real food nutritious in value for my new body hungers for purity and clean seed of the land. I no longer thirst of alcohol for I want clarity and somber spirit.

I do not want to cover up my true identity but to dance, for I am creatively boundless and have no need for pretend. Removing cigarette my habit of choice for they have I no need, no more. I need my lungs so I may breathe in, inhaling the bloom of roses, lilies, tulips . . . Calling out to all, who listen, no more will I pollute my lungs with harsh chemicals. I dare speak aloud and share my tidings.

Laughter with truth and play. Returning to my child, a natural high no longer do I need to run away but stay and play forever on a playground for all ages. Take out the toxicity from my body and cleanse my armor in lovingness for the beauty of the land I twirl my spirit again.

Clean air chanting to the heavens, away with toxic behavior and weak thought be no more for I will myself cleansed, thank you to God and his angels for being my strength, believing in me when I did not. No harm come to those who are brave in themselves and show their wounds proudly for I am a survivor of pain, misery, sorrow and abandonment and I still, stronger for I have turned my ill into love. For shame me no more I am renewed in my spirit, forgiven and I dare to love ever more.

Chemicals and Toxins

Food, alcohol, chemicals—for example, pesticides and cleaning products—in taking the body creates harmful and negative emotions. It destroys slowly like a plague. When you become in tune to what your body needs you will no longer be subject to these killers sensitive you will know what is right.

Be aware of their harmful ways and if they have warnings let that be your first clue.

Pay attention to what your body is telling you.

"Profit is gained where there is severe vulnerability."

Think, are you in control or have you given up your rights.

Be responsible for you and if you do depend on society or others take all that comes with.

Would you leave your child or pet with just anyone? If the answer is no then why would you leave yourself vulnerable to a society driven by greed and has zero impact on one's trust. The information you are given is not always the truth as it has been mentioned earlier the truth is in the hands of those who dare search it out for themselves.

If people lie to each other than how can we possibly trust consumers who profit in millions.

Ask yourself why are chemicals needed? What fears have been unleashed?

There are natural elements that do not harm. This is a personal matter for me and I have been just as guilty. So now I am being truly aware of what products I use and ask myself what can I do to make a positive difference.

I am not completely in a place to say I have never use chemicals but I now am thought conscious and using everyday household items. Taking the time and spending less money in using better elements that are safe and I feel better. It is a rewarding feeling and I love the fresh scents. From hair products to cleaning aids, supplements made of natural herbs. I am not 100 percent but I am getting there, creating balance.

To kill a weed that grows from the land know you are putting others livings things at risk.

Love is never lost once it is given life

Love evolves in consciousness and passion
Becoming the very air we breathe
Exhaling all despair and hate from my ego sense of self
In being I now feel the exoticness
ever bonding purity that my skin feels
the utter tenderness that only true love offers, in light.

My spirit healed, my being in tune with my heart
Connecting mind, body, and soul.

If you are going to be afraid to feel, you will never heal. We must face what fears us to move past the uncomfortable truth, in order to feel the sensation of love—allow it to teach us, touch us and grow us, flow through us. A healing cleanse. Love in its purest form, raw—it comes with all the emotions attached. It is up to us to identify with each of them and create unconditional love through feeling the pain. Understanding in truth. Have you ever loved in such a way you can feel the burn? Well if we put it into perspective, love is worth all that simply makes us real.

Our mind plays a role on our thoughts and creates dramas in which elude us from the truth. It can shift thought patterns. We must awaken and focus conscious thought into action. Next, cleanse our body, to see clarity—to know the difference. Stay in balance with the heart. If we are hurt with all our might move from that hurt, it will mold like a food. The mind will create chaos it will become like Endo (endometriosis) figure of speech if I may. Do not let it break down everything you love and hold dear. Killing your dreams.

So workout your love in such a way no matter how much you think impossible, you will always look good and feel good doing it. *Loving is key to living in balance.* Working out our body and heart and exercising our minds, staying present in every moment is imperative to healthy growth. A state of being in a true identity takes practice. You have the skills now just pursue ahead . . .

CHAPTER 13

Being Reborn

When the time comes when you decide to pursue something more within yourself, you will become detached from all you know.

Here is a prayer, may it show you courage.

Love Prayer
First, let me say thank you
I am not afraid for you I know are there
Always I have felt you
Please know I love you
From this moment on
I will come to need you more
Give me the strength and courage
For I now put all my trust in you
I want to know you for I want to know me
Show me the way . . .
Amen

Getting in touch with your kid at heart.

Keep free falling and love will open you up . . . Exercise your next move and stretch out that higher being.

Living a *lie* is *not* an option for me!

I choose to be a freak, weird, different, no longer will I be a fake, a robot, an impostor. Today I choose to be all in as the real me, it takes daily practice. I have to work at being the best of me, as everything in this life takes work and involves effort on the individual's part. It does get easier everyday. Bad days do happen I just no longer allow them to alter my agenda in what is right for me and ultimately those I come into contact with.

On your search for all that will feed your soul. Fill in what is missing; be brave for you are halfway there. You now enter life school and you choose the topic! Enjoy your search for the real meaning of life, who you are and what is the point of it all!

When the voices scream
to hate and judge,
I close my ears and breathe in with all my heart,
I love more and more
until all I am
is love
and the dark is no more.

An Epiphany

A memory took me on a daydream with my grama, sitting in fields of green and wildflowers in bloom.

On a beautiful day in the spring driving along a country road with some close friends.

On our way to a festival would be the very day I found myself realizing my true love for wildflowers, tall grasses that were as tall as I could reach. Closing my eyes and tuning out the voices . . .

"Sitting in her garden, smelling of dirt and enjoying the sound of her voice; I can still hear her, music to my ears. She was in essence perfect in nature and her love was a genuine leather. Nature trusted her kindness to the earth. I found it quite admirable and I found myself loving every moment spent with her, from mud bath pools made from the ground and worms as my best friends, I did not fear for they were life creating. Bugs, imagine these wondrous creatures and how detrimental they are for they share in beauty and feed the flowers that bloom, the trees that swarm our beautiful homes. We need them to better our earth.

Her fearless nature and tender heart, her laugh always had you laughing too, every time or at least made you smile back. My grama resembled God's love for she was faithful and dear. Confident in herself. Standing up for what she believed in and to those who tried to control her.

Coming back to, I thought how lucky a girl I am to have such an amazing woman in my life to implement truth, love and courage. So if you ask me what my favorite flower would be, a wildflower in bloom from the life of a weed I see all that is in color. My favorite person my grama, a yellow rose, as it was her very favorite and made her light up like heaven radiating the sun.

Can you think back to a time or person in your life that made such an impact on your life?

Are you or have been that person to someone?

Memories and Lost Love Remembered

There is a time for somewhere you will need to let go of a loved one's previous former self a loved one will be introduced to a soul remaining in the physical sense they need you to be understanding and accepting full of love they resist fearful energy.

This is NOT easy I am sure, you will need to be brave and learn how to attach yourself to the feeling of love and not the idea of who you knew them to be. By loving them outside of yourself. This is essential to the wellness of everyone involved.

I have studied this and being a medium intuitive, energy reader, and empath I feel this to be true. I have been in the company of people affected with these conditions and also been touched by it in my own family.

I am not an expert and their is always the exception of a few different severe cases, but overall I feel very connected and take this to heart, have you ever imagined the stress and obligation in being at max capacity in the responsibility of being who you are to others?

The sacrifice, the losses, also when one moves away from the light over time and their faith is disconnected from self and source. They have not found forgiveness or the understanding in what is true love. There is a process to go through . . . .

For one is never lost when love is present in thy heart.

In perspective, where we go when memory has left us. How the conditions of our once familiar story has collapsed with only broken pieces now, how frustration can and has affected families. "In our hearts we choose to go to a place where we remain happy and true."

When love was real, you can smell it in the air.

Alzheimer's disease is a struggle for families everywhere and as age and time persists so does frustration, and fear on many levels. But I assure you, it is evident that with love, faith, and belief in something more, "in remembering what is in the heart and not in the name."

"Begin again" where you find there is still HOPE in life, love, and friendship.

Demented one's thoughts become when we hold resentment in, old pain and sadness for fear will creep in and the dark will torment a Soul. We must replenish love, forgiveness and become one with the very present moment offer up ourselves in prayer and ask for a healing.

How you grow up and the world that has become made up of rules, obligations, and controlled environments.

Where is one left to go but back to the memories that are kept warm . . . a nice thought.

Photo by Michael Albright

An open heart cleanses a new sense of self with open arms. As an angel renews itself on this day. Allow the light to work through you, capture the essence, and open your eyes to see what is there in all moments. Feel the magic if you dare!

Do you ever wonder why we are *in love* with taking pictures of ourselves or in saving the moments in front of us?

Be Present in Love

I did not recognize my grandmother as sickly. It did not occur to me that she lost anything of her memories. It was the story she repeated several times that caught my attention, as if she was trying to get through a message. Was it me or herself she was convincing or sharing? I listened over and over for sometimes we miss the important parts, the first time.

To be honest, in general people have horrible attention spans and if they listen at all it is far in between. I have found in life and in my experiences that people are in such a hurry, and displaced in spirit that listening is as far removed as space. Too many times have I tried to get the attention of one I was sharing conversation, or a proud moment only to be ignored, mumbled off or *"oh, that's good, honey."* Are you serious?

This hearing—a sound and not listening to what it is someone is conveying lead me to become a woman who would make a life mission *in listening* to what it was people were trying to say or not say. My undivided attention would be a gift I would gladly give. So getting back to my grama, *I was patient* and loved hearing her voice. I can still hear it, the sound of her laugh tears me up in a most joyful way, *I can actually feel her!* I am grateful I paid attention.

Yes, she was outgoing, free-spirited, and heartfelt she was my favorite person! Her soul, timeless. Others thought her mad and crazy as hell. But did they ever truly dare to listen, were they ever so patient to truly take the time to know who she was—embarrassed some were, maybe jealous too, sadly. Some of her own children felt she was a disgrace. For she dressed not for others but herself. She was outspoken, no programmed spell. For her laughter was like bursts of evidence that the kid in her still remained.

True Love Replaced Her Memories

I recall a story she would tell a few times, I remember it well because it was when I first seen the dementia—as they would call it. I refer to it as memory restored because the thing is for every memory no longer needed, a new one, or old one emerges. You see there are times in our lives that we cover up, hide, or run from, we think we delete it but the time comes when our minds naturally recover and automatically begin to shift truth I see this very clearly for I am a Medium Intuitive, sensitive to "what is present" not fearing what others don't *want to know* or are *afraid to know.*

The story was of her late husband and in short he left her in a time; she was pregnant with her sixth child, my father. This man who in fact betrayed his family and himself for hurt he caused, may in true lead to my grandmother storing it away. There was a time he tried to make peace and come back, but with all her strength, willed him away. My grams not one for easy forgiveness, *like many.* When it came to outside our intermediate family, of course. Some thought of her as cold but I believe it was her huge heart, she had to protect it, for how much pain can one person take?! Dementia would speak these words aloud though **my memory plays it like this;** with an intense glare and sincere presence, it captivated me in a way, anyway this is what she said "*I forgive my husband and still, I love him.*" Those very words, I declare!

A few times over the months that passed she repeated, again. I knew the time was coming her life she was mending, for heaven would take her soon and this thought killed me, had me up many a nights. But it was in my heart to listen to her and for her to say she loved him and forgave him. *A miracle not an illness* was apparent to me, clearly she was conscious for she was brave enough to go where we fear—to forgive and love unconditionally.

So do not try to keep your loved ones for they are brave to wonder, the Spirit knows better. "Be love" and not control for they love you so. Listen to them, laugh with them but do not pity them and worse feel despair for yourself. Frustration you may feel but in sincerity and true, love is all there really is. Grow with love, for change is evident, it will come so let it in and welcome *truth, forgiveness,* and *faith.*

Be not afraid for memories "our truth there was love" now love remains in place when memories no longer are clear, no trace of who you are.

"Love thy older person for their stories are true."
You, will one day be an older version looking back.
What will your story be and what will you represent?

Yellow Rose

A rose halo in the brightest of yellow
her scent carries with her, sweet
she shined a coat of earth her posture straight an arrow
heaven could not miss her she stood for
nature and everything good
She would represent love, strength and truth
for every yellow rose honors her name
Yolanda Mary

Grandmas and Grandpas
are all so special
to be loved by them and to love them,
be proud for you are not old but wise and true.
For youth is in the heart of the strong,
Believers
being brave in who they are
proud their stories that captivate
the hearts and minds of the young.

Photo taken by Michael Albright

Therapy in Nature and in the Beach

To be born again amongst the Sun, my grams delighted in the warmth of the sun, the sand in her toes and how the water carried her . . . the back float being her favorite swim as she would connect with the blue sky above.

143

Heaven shined through the pillow white cotton shaped clouds where the angels sat upon watching over us.

"A man who thinks himself wealthy in nature knows himself better than the man still searching for treasure of silver and gold."

Finding comfort in Nature rather it be camping, walking, swimming in the lake or ocean . . . Having the dirt at your feet taking it in with your hands and smelling the soil its purity offering to you what is of the land that is ever so kind, healing and growing is for your pleasure and living free. For to swim in a lake or ocean how it wraps you with its loving hugs there is something familiar, something comforting. The sand and how it works as a natural exfoliant. Sometimes reminding oneself that our answers are secrets in the land . . . at our feet and above our heads only to those who take notice and pay attention. If you have not realized this truth, know it offers itself up to you, take heart, will you not?

Some cannot afford the luxuries in life but I am here to tell you, all you have to do is look outside yourself and the cost is, in taking notice. Be brave in your search for the small discoveries are within your reach.

"For traveling through time I found loved ones thinking of me, praying for me and now I am ready to move on."

A love letter

My vow is this, my love, on this day onto tomorrow, I will honor "you" as my fellow. For all I have is thy love in my heart and respect for you as a man with integrity, kindness, and bravery. In all our will, here we stand side by side. Clever the Gods are for all we are is; hope for it be treasured and reassured always, that love may it continue to grow. Let us create a garden of life and tend to it daily for when we need, its nourishments will refresh, renew and remind us always it is love still tis that it exists.

You set a light in me and I for you for sharing in the endeavor of man and wife we may never be lost from each other for a candle be lit in me and in you. I promise this I, shall always remember the trueness of why we are and why is simply. I love you, admire you and I, my dearest I am proud to be.

I will honor your name as you have honored my free spirit . . . For it excites me to begin our adventure together!

The love that brings out the very best in you. To renew you in a deeper sense. To care for you in a way you need to grow and to heal from your long journey thus far. It has been my experience that truly liking myself is important. The love I have given to others has supplied me in comfort and nourished me from the inside. Loving with all I had to give never holding back. If you ask me, *have I felt love in return,* I would reply *Yes!* Many times over. Yet I cannot at this time speak of a soulful love.

I have shared, it is my personal love for God that surrounds me today. This stage of my life is dedicated to him, through understanding and loving my sacred self. I know him on a deep and intimate level, feeling more connected than ever before. Through meditation is where he comes through, naturally for me.

An unselfish love eager to discover their purpose in the patience of another. A prince who rescues his princess and therefore his honor is restored. In good faith, they begin to grow encouragement for all town.

For do I still believe in the fairy tale . . . ? Abso-fucking-lutely!

Let me express my feelings on swear words. It is my belief that to fully express or animate oneself sometimes it takes words that will turn heads, get attention, point across. It just feels right ever since I was a baby the words flowed outward, the F word was one of my favorites. My parents would suggest pretty strongly if you must swear do it without anger and abuse to another. We were told use the F word before you ever dare use the N word!

They taught me to respect others and take responsibility for my choices and actions, meaning use swear words in a positive manner, if we must use them at all. Now this does not mean they encouraged us to swear but they were realistic and knew eventually we would, so they ambulated to care for the very words spoken true would be the moral.

CHAPTER 14

Insanity

Insanity: doing the same thing over and over
again expecting different results.
—Famous quote by Albert Einstein

This was passed on to me when I really needed answers and help healing. It would help in moving on from an ugly place of despair. It took years of saying it aloud or in my head, writing down in plain words to see and still it did not come to me till I was ready to do the hard work that was ahead. I want to thank this special someone for little does he know he was *my sponsor, my mentor, my friend, and my love.*

Do not kid yourself this is an addiction, insanity that is. Connecting mind, body, and soul is a lifestyle. A change in your chemistry it is not to be taken lightly but with all seriousness. Think of yourself as an addict. You must deprogram from all you know, think, been told. The pain that is very real in all the habits that become toxic. Be aware if you need help there is someone out there just ask in prayer, you don't have to believe at first just have to want it bad enough!

Do you fight to win or do you fight to stay sane?

Coming undone feelings of pain, her soul restless what is she to do, crying inside, not a soul to know the bothersome of loss, contempt in her shame, how shall she go on?

How long will one go on ranting about how horrible life is? Can you only imagine that once you truly ask for it to *stop*, and I mean with all of your heart, mind, and soul. It will. Would you "believe" that you just might have more say than you think . . . .

There truly, really, really **is** magic that happens in just one thought, the ingredients in having a better life are closer with daring yourself forward. The tools are within your reach, I promise.

> I want to *scream* at the chaos and ignorance
> feeling like I want to leave this place
> what is the point everywhere you look heart-
> break sales and ads too
> from positive to negative
> what the hell is this madness i am subjected to?!
> Lost souls roaming the halls
> they are sad and don't know what to do.

Do not give up because the hard part is letting you know, you are strong enough to get through. It is only one chapter of your story. Think of it as stream of movement, do you believe it would be worth it?

Movement is beautiful, keep moving, and when you need to stop, do. It is not easy when things fall apart or when we lose loved ones, jobs, and so on. So there's a thunder cloud let it rain baby and dance and dance to your own beat, cultivate a plan and change your channel, frequent the storm may vary.

But know if you do choose to pray, an angel will carry you through. A friend, a love or even a stranger or two, they will be there in goodness but know it is a chapter in your story so, be the hero, the victim, the survivor or the star. Your choice, this my friend is the value in accepting yourself as a winner, never a loser.

For a loser may be one that is lost yet never are they forgotten.

"All of our broken hearts mended unto a garden of hearts blooming in love together a garden."

Ripping at my skin, I feel imprisoned in.
Looking into the mirror at an image I do not recognize.
What game is being played am I it's joker
for this place I dwell is filled with strangers
who call themselves friends
HA—Brief memories of good times
but the reality is all the lies lived
and I another one told.
Have I done this to myself again and again?
Is anyone out there who I can trust
for I cannot even tell the truth
from my tongue is tied and my heart is bleeding red
I can see the blood running through my veins.
I know myself to be alive but why is it I want to die.
To live, what does that even mean?

I beg for I am trapped with criminals as my peers *feelings of dread torment my very inner being.*

What is it about time that makes it almost impossible to concentrate?

Loyalty, commitment, honesty, integrity. These words with their definitions will follow as you keep reading through. The chaos, hostages, and what happens when we allow these words to invade or perhaps we need to explore the meaning once again. Our truth, our relationships are at risk. How have we become so distorted and manipulated? Have we construed the wrong ideas?

Like the Bible it must be read in clarity, words open up to us when we are ready to listen with pure of heart, intention. Thinking for ourselves is imperative to understanding the truth. Different for us all yet the same for those ready to go there.

Loyalty is a beautiful thing but when does being loyal make us lose yourself in beliefs, needs, how far does one go for loyalty before they sacrifice their Soul, Spirit and eventually our happiness within?

We all need a friendly reminder from time to time, more in definition and meanings along this way.

I feel the need to add definition to the words of wisdom for the meanings have become lost. We all need reminders. When you go to school you are subject to learning. When you graduate you are responsible to continue your education. It took me awhile to understand the real meaning, the point to it, well here it tis. Everything changes like the season, *"history in the making."* As we evolve so do words, our vocabulary enriches as our mind develops. We must continue to grow, educate ourselves, seek understanding open our hearts to reasoning of pure intent, truer meanings than those given or should I say showed, to us.

In our own way we can account for more than a dollar which will not pay for your life in love and friendship.

Loyalty [loi-uh l-tee]

Sound it out and listen to the beat of the word what it means to be loyal, what it represents.

The state or quality of being loyal; faithfulness to commitments or obligations. What makes one obligated? The word is subjective to, harsh, and vulnerability to control.

Faithful and true to someone you care for and respect.

Be a leader, a man with fierce loyalties—be cautious of those with Ego attached.

"I did not see where this definition said be loyal to man. That is our choice or someone who expects that of us."

"Loyalty is a royal word I feel and it should be in the hands of someone who is faithful and kind, grateful for such trust and friendship."

For no man be under such obligation that he loses himself his beliefs of what is true, no man should lose himself to control of another, to be obligated to know one word or person but to his own integrity and love for what is good what is right.

Faithful is one who believes in another, so I will be someone whom looks out for the best intent.

The Rut: the day to day maintenance, lack of play, lack of energy, tone displaced. Low inspirational vibes. Dry sense of being. Dark and dim light

The Blues: feelings of sadness, loss sometimes just a flat line in rhythm a time to ponder, be still.

Emotional constipation causes depression, overeating, under eating, addiction, neglect of self, anxiety, anger, anal retentiveness, OCD, it desensitizes you in one way replaces good sense with bad sense in sensitizes in negative harmful ways. Addictions of all sorts. Negative energy Backed up aggression, in need of more love, forgiveness, courage.

Is this you? We all feel them from time to time. Don't let them occupy too much of your precious time. When mine come around I sit still depending on the necessary act. Have I overdone it, spread myself too thin? Maybe let the negative energy in? Whatever the case trust in God to make haste with all ugh feelings of taboo away, with you! Start fresh after a good long nap, take a bubble bath, or workout at the gym. Take up that art project that has been staring at you. A good medicine might be saying hey friends I need you, an angel, a mother, a neighbor or brother someone please just look up and say I need *help*!

Linger here for too long and you shall be lost. What you ingest internally like food, drink and chemicals may cause hormonal stress and moodiness. By eating, smelling or merely your environment of negativity will cause you disease. Your tears set them free, if happiness, sadness has built up, been held up for whatever the reason waiting to rain on you, *let the thunder roll and enjoy the storm*. The sun will come to shine on you after.

Abused by the innocence of those whom are blind to the control of those they have come to trust. Therefore trust has been manipulated, bent, misconstrued! Do not blame those whom have crossed you for they are subject to bad behaviors and intent in the wrong behaviors for they may not have been taught, lead in the wrong direction. Understanding why and taking responsibility in following the leader.

No real harm done just be aware of your circumstances and surroundings. It is beautiful to have loyalty but it should not under no faithful being, be taken advantage of someone's trust. In truth, it only steers us away from each other and creates holes where there should be depth of soul. I am loyal to myself and to God and when I give my loyalty to another I first tune in and observe their intentions, ask myself are they filled with a hidden agenda or false promise, feeling for the right answer I then proceed to trust myself to go further.

"Through loyalty trust is built or broken. Treasure those whom honor your worth and give loyalty the respect it deserves."

Conquer Your Fears

- Love
- Guilt
- Shame
- Anger
- Sadness
- Loneliness
- Anxiety
- Weight Issues
- Your True Greatness

Get Your Heart Right!

Walk that walk be true to your sacred self, be not afraid of failure and loss it is a farce! No man shall fail in his truth intent, be mindful for you in him are perfectly flawed, timeless and right. Succeed in trying to go farther than you fear, walk the talk, voice love and act. Proceed to the finish line where you are set free to be whomever you choose only set them free.

"Never should we be ashamed of our failures for without them how would we know how great we can be. Rise and believe you are sure to succeed in everything you do, with heart and good intent know the road ahead is paved just for you, just one catch you have to walk it alone."

Left at Home with Anxiety

"A Positive Vent"

My friend's baby shower was Saturday and I truly did plan on going, but sadly, I had to decline. I am just not ready for crowds and stress brings on pain, so I let her know, as she is always understanding. *"I am thankful for good friends."*

Coming to grips with reality and truth about this condition, is freedom I need. I love people it is my business to be social and connected. I am a Life Coach, among other things and I have knowledge in areas of wellness. So being taken out sometimes is a drag and makes me feel helpless. Visiting social media home place and seeing photos of my friends sharing in on the fun and exciting time made me realize Endo and it's accomplish anxiety have stolen my life.

On the flip side, there is always a most positive for me, as you will find. In being sick I have been given a gift, to sit back, be still and make a choice to find what it tis that Shanna can do now, in place of being active and working outside my home at this time. I prayed on it and the next thing I knew I was writing, and painting again, hobbies I have not been in touch with for a while. Maybe God has a plan for me after all and slowing me down would help me see things differently.

My condition is not stealing my life but giving me a newer version of self, so I may be better than I once was. Therefore I will understand others on a deeper level. My compassion and understanding are growing, I can truly feel what it is to love. *"I will be patient with myself and this condition and not ever let it destroy me but build me up through Perseverance and Faith."* I am stronger than the illness. Venting out loud helps, too!

My love for anyone suffering from anxiety or an illness. "Be love."

Commitment (k*uh*–**mit**-M*uh*nt)

Be aware of those who will *commit you* to bend at their will.

A state where one may be committed

The act of committing, engaging, pledging

An engagement; Involvement

A promise

Obligation: The feeling of being obligated against our will. Do not promise yourself in such a way or ask another to be obligated for if the intention is good but need to be let out careful not to put asunder a man.

To promise to pay your bills on time.

To have a sincere commitment to a religion etc.

"Without sincerity there is no good to come to hold a loved one hostage by a word. Give it life for he who has good intention be free from such penalty."

To imprison one to their word.

To honor your commitment.

If one asks to be free of such a commitment honor them. For each man be responsible for their own integrity and promise. Life is ours to be had, consequence comes to those without good intention and lack of love and honor.

Let it be known people and times change.

"Before making such commitment honor thy truth."

Promise (*prom-is)*

A declaration that something will or will not be done or given.

Expression, assurance, on which expectation is based.

promises to uphold

153

indication of what may be expected.

Don't make a promise you can't keep.

future excellence or achievement

a writer who holds promise.

something that is promised—joining business venture, marriage, -vows of honor

to engage or undertake

Can we afford the let down, disappointment of not keeping a simple promise to a child, a loved one. Ask yourself why did you not keep your promise, was it worth it.

A promise is a gift, a secure offering to self or another.

To make one is safe keeping.

He said he would never cheat again, this is too complex without truth to oneself this promise is subject to change, it might be upheld with heart. The person promised is responsible therefore. The one who promises such a thing needs to think before throwing up the word I promise not to ever cheat again. Take account of your feelings, emotions, truth, and heart on the matter. Be true with promise to yourself first then you can promise in good faith.

Trust is built from the truth we tell ourselves and come to believe.

Friend (frend)

A person drawn to another by feeling, affection

Personal regard for another

Someone who honors another's space

to share love, faith, friendship, life, similar likes,

A trusted confident

Family without blood ties

Connection of souls, spirits

A gift, to cherish

A friend to play, talk, work with

To be a good friend is to honor respect another for who they are to bring out the best in them simply by being their friend.

A friend is not to be controlled, become jealous of or judged for if you betray a friend is to commit fraud, remember a friend is one who cares, loves, admires, believes in you. Naturally they come to trust you and to break that is to have consequence.

I will not suffer the penance for friendships are dear to me each and everyone I carry in my heart.

A friend, is someone to share intimate details of our life and share in on our travels with love. A friend someone whom to laugh, cry and vent our most private fears. To share a crazy—like laugh, to simply role play in thoughts of being just that fun loving kid!

Do you remember him or her, your childlike self?

When we grow up we leave our child behind, mainly because they tell us we should for all adults claiming this is what it is! Some of us wishing to be grown up but only because we want a sense of self, not to be controlled and displaced like our parents and guardians.

"We are only children with grown up mistakes."

For look up to God and he will make you young again, be wild and free running through fields of green or painting on the steps, what was that favorite game you used to play? Throwing the ball in the middle of the street with all the guys before you would split into threes.

Furthermore may I add what possesses a friend the best of to come undone? Lose sight of the tower of promise, love and loyalty. Why does one whom swears her dying breath she will take with her your most special secrets. Is it for us to give to a higher source? Is it a test of will? Whatever the true case may be, I believe with such betrayal of friendships gone bad, the ill of unhappiness, the jealousy, the insecurity, the feeling of one losing the tight bond when others come close and it is no longer just the two.

I am one whom has been betrayed too many times but I have come to forgive. I do not forget our friendship for what is true is. I am learning to forget the wrong that was done unto me. It has no place where I live today. I send my love to these friends and know without a doubt their intentions were just for they were not true to themselves but weak in place where fear creeps. A voice that carried their actions.

We are not perfect just hurt from the hard lessons that invades our happy homes.

Jealousy is a disease that is crushing to one's soul and it steals the life of those you hold most dear. It has a deceiving urge to destroy, it is a hallucinogenic drug in its breath for when it whispers nothings in your ear, if you are not pure of heart it can reap your soul and twist every sane thought from your consciousness and your will, fallen. A tornado effect will havoc your life and those you have hurt will be lost to you forever.

Keep the promise to yourself. A Pedestal no one should be put on one, except for the greatness of God. We need to understand who we are and understand before making such promises to another before ourselves and those whom ask of us plenty for we are all guilty of.

Jealousy, insecurity and anger *kills*—be brave in who you are for all that is good.

If you fail to be a tower of good but want to be better, than simply seek out help and change for the better. It is a win-win!

A man must climb the mountain and a woman must seek thirst from his lips for a child who is there to guide them from themselves.

Love may it imprint on your soul here and now till you reach eternity in forever.

Love (luhv)
Love is . . .

A tender, profoundly passionate affection for another being.
A feeling.
A warm personal attachment or deep affection.
Sexual, sensual, desire.
Beloved, sweetheart, darling, *Amore*
Used in direct contact as a term of endearment, affection

A love affair of the hearts
Sexual as an act, intimate as an emotion
To love, to be loved . . . .
A state of being
A strong liking.
To take pleasure in
A need. To benefit from love simply by giv-
ing it, sharing it, embracing it in its raw nature.
We need love to grow, to evolve.
Embrace and kiss someone to share love
through such intimate space.
A hug may suggest love as it also can heal love.
Consideration, Gratefulness, to give mercy,
Darkness eluded by pain and misfortune.
Emotional neglect will trigger addictive behaviors.
Habit forming ideas steal creative thought.
Approach your negative self and be straight
Tough love is needed to break barrier of content.

To overcome constant sadness one must walk the passage
through discovering-said; Truth and sacred self.

CHAPTER 15

Creative Energy

Crying out for some infinite majestic inspiration.

Love and reasoning.

Allow your intuition to guide you. *Trust in it!!*

When I find myself nervous and my thoughts are all over the place, I have found utter peace in creating or working on art projects. Rather it is painting, drawing, writing or even cleaning my space. It distracts from the noise in my head or around in my environment and before I know it I am calm again and I have even created something out of haste go figure my energy was trying to tell me something and I listened by doing something constructive and for me. It changes all perspective and sets the tone for greatness, a time ago, I could have gone mad or got in a load of drama from such emotion. Now, not being a big fan and having my fill of negative consequences, I throw myself into positive action. I found I have passions that need my attention. I finished paintings and give it away as a gift.

You are not useless and nothing needs to be perfected. Just dive in and dare to explore your world within. Being idle for too long can and will self-destruct in nature. Unplug from everything when you find yourself coming undone in, and plug into your sacred self if it is drawing, fishing, reading, taking a bath, crocheting, making car models, journaling, and working out. Take a class, volunteer, take a walk, or make a long distance call. It has been a while since you have channeled your needs. I know you are good at something, so do it! I did, and I am thrilled it is all coming back to me. I am as a child, and in the comfort of my child-like spirit, I can feel her again. I thought she was gone forever.

PS: If you did not have a good childhood, you did, there was a time when before you knew better and the hard lessons came, a spirit that lives in. You were born of love into a world that needed you, that is why you are here, spite good, bad, wonderful, or even the ugly. Trust me, you are a child of love, and you are meant to be happy. If you are reading this, you are meant for something even if it be small in your size. You are important; please begin again. Time is of the essence the garden needs your tending to.

Start planting seeds . . . .

What are your passions? Do you have hobbies?

What makes you happy now?

What made you happy ten years ago?

What did you want to be, as a child, as young as you can remember?

What will make you happy in twenty years?

Are you bored, tired of people telling you what to do and how to do it? Okay then, *take responsibility* and do not just float through life having a bad attitude or worse doing the job required of you, less than and by the way who said you have only one talent and you have to stay at the same job, work the same career for the rest of your life. Times change, we evolve and we sometimes have more than one task ahead of us. Never believe the tale, this is your life live with it. Every obligation should be looked at as an opportunity, I heard that somewhere and it is brilliant, is it not? Be in the moment true and do what is necessary of you, do it to the very best of your ability, *in good spirits.* If you are at a point in your life where you have noticed you want more and you feel it is the time to explore a career or something special it is that you want, do you need more passion in your life?

Putting love into everything and the smallest of things is the righteous idea, acting it out with pleasure is humbling. Like seeding a garden, plants need water. Personally, I always have had love and suspect some people will come to learn. Adding love is the special ingredient you need to make a delicious cake. Well take that ingredient and add some of your own concoction. If you are at the present time working at a fast food restaurant, or perhaps assisting to your dream job, you get my point.

Think of this job as a benefit to your life resume. Each and every moment in this job, be present, and care about your work. *Without you it would not be a complete circle.* Your task is important but if in fact you want more and again you are tired of being told you're not good enough. Look in the mirror no job is superior to another person you need to understand, intricate reality in making it count and from there you will elevate higher.

Without laziness, excuses, ignorance, and arrogance. Put forth positive, spirited, and care into your work. Look in the mirror and *be love.* That negative tune you have playing in your ear, replace it with creative sounding music. I promise you if you take for one moment and realign yourself make some positive changes, for you! Life will begin to express gratitude your way and respond positively and move you closer to your calling, dream, ideal workspace. I speak from experience and love. Be humble in your work for if it was not for you, others would feel the empty gap. Stop crying and sulking, wishing and hoping is simply not enough, create a better tomorrow through connecting mind, body, and soul.

As you develop your new improved awareness so does your vocabulary evolve. Your body now responds better with less food and more nutrition you are lighter so your physical self needs different food, drink more water. Your taste buds will change your senses are higher, sensitive to taste, smell and the air quality itself, your intuition is evolving. Attitude, likes, dislikes. Practice mindfulness, your mind needs cleansing. Your chemistry, overall health, and wellness will begin to alter in a positive way. This change derives bountiful measures. New words emerge from your lips. Meet unto your new self and start living free within the light of love.

In act of hobbies, unwrapping my gifts, exploring my talents, finding explicit wonder in doing absolutely nothing. Appreciating nature.

The changes I arrive to bring me closer to the truths, it is when I notice the beauty and eternal life in nature again, that I begin to *ignite* my creative side. Daring myself forward and out loud!

S.O.L.: you may remember this as "shit out of luck"! No more—I pronounce these three beautiful letters now known for "smiling out loud" admit it we need more positive and more smiling! SOL

M.O.V.Y.: Happy Motivation, yearning for motivation, are you? Get your MOVY on!

It does not always have to make sense it just has to be authentic.

Have fun and make it count from this moment on!
Look forward to your life and all that will unfold with being love.

What will your new words, ideas, creative energy reveal through you?

In celebrating you . . .

I am late but never are you forgotten . . . . Happy birthday to a soul with love thus reigns upon all the visions of white in which circle only pure undying rivers of enlightenment, may you know your beauty in light of love.

"Never be afraid to glorify your awesome self come to trust a knowing deep down. You are deserving, whatever the circumstance, this is a chance to make things right in one way or another. To know in true, you matter. In clarity only do we then begin to see ourselves as part of the universe, and we become whole again as one."

CHAPTER 16

Understanding the True Meaning of Death

For parting is sweet sorrow.
—Shakespeare,
Romeo and Juliet, 2.2.184

Death and my interpretation, in short.

In passing through one dimension through onto another, evolving in Spirit, an expansion in imagination, truth and thus the whole meaning of life, love and being. To die is to shed one skin for a richer version of eternal life.

My Promise

Making every moment count. Inspiring hope, love, and compassion to all whom seek out. Writing, speaking, and living the raw and beautiful truth. Living the life God wants for me and while I have been hurt I still have a beating heart that loves more now than I ever knew was possible. An open heart loves true. For the secrets of my soul whisper healing notes and I am again free to live happily within my Sacred self touching those with inspirational thoughts that soon turn to light.

Let death not be taken from one whom loves true, honor thy spirit for it lives free in you.

A child's love within holding O thy mother true.

The wings of a fellow

bring life to one

whom has moved unto the light

Only to bestow love in a new and vivacious way

To awaken in color

for the very love of a mother

Look, for I am by your side,

loving you, being strong for you

For I am thy fellow.

Bringing life and warranty
to a loved one who has lost sleep
from their sadness and worry
I assure you as the rain cleanse the morn
I will be back again, in a dream, in the very corner of your eye
do not doubt for I whisper in your ear
and nestle calm in your being
next time you feel a tickle
fresh from the autumn air.
Know it is I.

I feel quite confident on this subject matter for I am, a medium intuitive and have accepted my gifts and continue to grow and embrace my abilities, as a life coach. Taking in my spiritual awareness and coming to understand myself and others more through experience, real life experience with those whom are living and whom have passed on.

I was finding that I could without trying connect to someone on a most intimate and personal level. In session I would come to reach them on a spirit realm and learned I could not only commute with my client on a level but be reached by their loved ones past.

Even those whom still embody their earthly selves physically, they were able to detach to their spirit self and were able to reach me on a higher level to relate messages to their loved ones. I will never forget my first Spirit whom came to me and how it felt. How he was able to convey such peace and happiness to his family . . . through me, a healing that would mend in time, an understanding that was so desperately needed so they may move on with their lives, true, free of pain and have peace from unanswered questions. A forgiveness that has lifted the family from angst. His spirit since has transcended light unto his passing.

I walk the earth with wings of a dove, my soul leading me to the sound of footsteps walking the halls restless and disheartened for do not weep for I am not gone, just free, so talk to me. Do not fear in what you may not understand, feel from your heart and trust in God. For he carried me here, believe in serenity faithful is the heart who is awake.

It is the living who suffer the loss, for those who move on are very much alive and well.

No harder truth then the loss of a loved one. Heartbreak that feels like death has replaced a sense of living, go within and pray for understanding and disconnect from what you know, plug into spirit and allow your faith to be instilled renewed in you for pray to see, the light and visit the unknown.

In love thy thoughts be true for tis life renewed in one death merely a flower blooms in place.

Be aware of those whom provoke fear unto death. The meaning to die *is* misunderstood.

Revel in the knowing there is no death to one who loves in truth.

I do not believe we die and we are no more. I believe in everlasting life in the miracle of moving on to a better being, living, thriving in open waters of love, it is not us who suffer from death only those we leave behind who feel the loss and remorse. My promise when I leave this place is to take with me the misconception of what it truly means to live and that there is no loss in death for there is no such meaning to die forever.

Remember the string that connects to us all and then there is mirrored reflections of ourselves in others.

My grama left us for a better world in the summer of 2006. She visits me, continues to guide me, protect me and love me. She is free and roams the earth in light, love and in color.

I know I walk with the angels as they are always there for me. If you need your angel, simply ask.

You did not imagine it as a child for truth has always been there. No longer look away from what imagination has in store for you. Make believe all over again and dance in fun and glory.

I woke from a dream last night and you were there asking me;
where have you been, I answered with a smirky smile . . . never
was I gone from your side just is, changed my appearance.

Making Room for the Light

What makes me do what I do?

Most of my life, in time, I followed my heart and trusted my gut! Doing so lead me exactly where I intended to be. Some may think indifferent of me maybe to ease their hurt or inexperience on the matter for choices I have made, yet here I speak the truth.

Love, my passion. It being all that I am. I have felt the innocence of love. The purity, it remains in me even now throughout all the pain and loss. Igniting in me my purpose, the reason I dwell.

I want to help those who have lost hope, or forgotten why they are here and most important of all, to enlighten, so they come to know and acknowledge how extraordinary, beautiful and intelligent they are and that it resides in them no matter how lost, dark, hurt or alone they become.

Truth is what secures me to continue on remains the same. I have a fire inside, pressing me to always move forward and keep moving. I have a longing for something amazing and I know without a shadow of a doubt—it is to be true. I will continue to inspire, bring hope and help others find peace and truth, so they may generate it daily in their own lives. All is depending on self to heal our inner sacred being. For I may not be perfect nor innocent, just one whom has awaken.

What makes me do what I do is choosing to be an example. I have come to love my life and found incredible gratefulness for all whom have been a part of it. They helped condition me, for better or worse. I stand tall and assure others to aspire and break the wrong behaviors and to enlighten the idea, Heaven is on earth. I, no human nor I me, yet who I am is to be revealed through my story.

We all have one and I believe through sharing mine, others will come to be proud of theirs, not ashamed nor afraid. Without pain there is no glory to be known. In other words, "a true love story."

The love story is our own story. I, as it was intended one as it remains "the One" all the same. Life is good and it should be lived . . . . told and then the power will be restored from within and fear will expire, no longer holding us hostage. Imagine living free from guilt, prejudice, random thoughts in which elude us from happiness. Imagine being truly happy, to wake each morning looking forward to a new adventure, a new beginning. Confront yourself and allow you to animate what you came here for.

Photo taken by Shanna

If your future self asked you right now, what is the very meaning of your life, and what is missing from your life what would your response be?

To be continued by you . . .

Enjoy your journey, each moment, and make it count.
Sending you warm sunlit hugs and moonlight kisses, blessings from my heart to yours.

"Bringing heart in connecting mind, body, and soul."

See you soon in the midway of love.

ABOUT THE AUTHOR

Shanna Rebis was born and raised in Rochester, New York. She became a licensed cosmetologist and has been self-employed most of her career. Taking small jobs has kept her humble and involved with people. Her passion for love inspires her to observe. Writing has always been a way for her to express herself and use as a tool to attain her goals. Through seeking out more experiences and endeavors, she has continued to trust her gut and follow her heart when it comes to business and relationships, which has led her to meet many different people and learn new ways to live. After a time of spiritual change and growth, Shanna used her experiences to build a career as a holistic life coach. She expanded her consciousness through meditation, taking in nature and finding the meaning of what death truly means in its entirety. Shanna has always considered herself a deep person. She now has the knowledge to channel her energy to understanding exquisite truth. When she fell sick, she dared herself to write a book. *Poetic LOVE Frenzy* is her first published collection of poetry and prose. Shanna currently lives in an area of Florida that is South with her family.

Special thanks to photographer Lauren F. Stirpe for Author's Photo

CPSIA information can be obtained
at www.ICGtesting.com
Printed in the USA
FSOW03n1807020117
29035FS

9 781683 484561